19 traditional patterns for a new
generation of generous quiltmakers

By **Joanne Larsen Line**
Story text by Jeff Brumbeau
Illustrations by Gail de Marcken

Orchard Books ◆ New York
An Imprint of Scholastic Inc.

Grateful acknowledgment is made to the following for granting permission to reprint copyrighted material:

Martingale & Co for the quilt term glossary (page 144 and inside back cover) and diagram (inside front cover) adapted from Simply Scrappy Quilts at Patchwork Place, from the books *Simply Scrappy Quilts* (1995) and *Two Color Quilts* (1998) by Nancy J. Martin.

Library of Congress Cataloging-in-Publication Data
Line, Joanne Larsen, 1937-
More Quilts From The Quiltmaker's Gift / Joanne Larsen Line; illustrations by Gail de Marcken; story text by Jeff Brumbeau. — 1st Scholastic ed. p.cm.
ISBN 0-439-51951-9 (pbk.)
1. Patchwork — Patterns. 2. Quilting — Patterns. I. De Marcken, Gail. II. Brumbeau, Jeff. Quiltmaker's gift. III. Title. TT835.L5397 2003 746.46'041 — dc21
2002044994

10 9 8 7 6 5 4 3 2 1   03 04 05 06 07

Printed in the U. S. A.   24
First Scholastic edition, September 2003

Dedication

To my husband, Roy, who for over forty years,
in good times and in bad, has been my partner, friend, and lover.

To Dale, whose commitment, creativity, and enthusiasm
makes him the son every parent dreams of.

And in memory of my son Bruce, who has taught me
that time heals a broken heart and whose spirit lives on
in the beautiful memories he created.

—*Joanne*

Special thanks to

Joy Morgan Dey, whose computer graphics skills and artistic vision
are evident in every page of this book.

Barb Engelking, Claudia Clark Myers, Judy Stingl Timm, and Kim Hoffmockel
Wells, who worked with me in developing the unique interpretations of
All Kinds, Cobweb, Tea Leaf, and Fish.

Lila Taylor, technical editor for *American Patchwork & Quilting* magazine,
who painstakingly reviewed all the fabric requirements, cutting instructions,
and piecing diagrams for accuracy.

Susan Gustafson, whose keen eyes and orderly mind have caught my errors.

Jeff Brumbeau, whose charming fable inspires the creative energies
of all who read it.

Gail de Marcken, whose incredible imagination is abundantly evident
in her artwork and in the secret stories behind her illustrations.

Dee Wojciehowski, whose computer skills added much to the book.

Barbara Brackman, for her systematic cataloguing and differentiating of quilt
patterns by block construction in her *Encyclopedia of Pieced Quilts Patterns*.

The many quilters from Minnesota and Wisconsin who first loved
The Quiltmaker's Gift and who generously made miniquilts for the traveling
trunk show, created full-size quilts for this book, and tested and retested
the pattern instructions.

Amy Griffin, Senior Editor, for her understanding, kindness, and patience.

And finally, to Don and Nancy Tubesing, whose creative imaginations
selected *The Quiltmaker's Gift* from the thousands of manuscripts they
received each year. This book promotes and celebrates generosity and the
joy of giving and is making a positive impact on everyone who
comes in contact with it.

Contents

Introduction

This book is the second companion book to *The Quiltmaker's Gift*, an inspiring fable about a mythical quiltmaker, who made the most beautiful quilts in the world—then gave them away to the poor and homeless.

When a greedy king demands a quilt of his own, imagining it will make him happy as none of the many treasures in his castle have, the quiltmaker refuses. For this impudent rejection, the king throws her to a hungry bear and strands her on a tiny island, but each time the quiltmaker's kindness thwarts his plans.

Ultimately she relents and agrees to make a quilt for the king, but only on one condition—he must give away all his possessions to the poor. Eventually he does so, and *The Quiltmaker's Gift* concludes with a powerful message about the joy of giving.

The Quiltmaker's Gift was a huge success selling over 200,000 copies in a little over a year. *Quilts from The Quiltmaker's Gift* was written in response to many requests for the quilt patterns illustrated in the picture book. It, too, was very well received, selling 50,000 copies in the first ten months on the market. Both books have won honors and awards. *The Quiltmaker's Gift* was on the *New York Times* Best Sellers list for over a year, and many journal and newspaper articles were written about the two books. The authors and illustrator of both books traveled extensively in the past two years, making speaking engagements and radio and television appearances on local and national shows. Often the first question asked during the question-and-answer segment of each program is, "When will the other patterns be available?"

This book brings you nineteen new patterns. You will find this book similar to the first book but with several enhancements.

Joanne signs books and shows quilts for *More Quilts from The Quiltmaker's Gift* in Hackensack, MN.

The yardage needed for borders is listed separately, and the instructions have been written specifically for the featured quilt.

Beginners will appreciate easy-to-sew patterns made entirely of squares and triangles. For the more experienced, there are patterns using diamonds, hexagons, curved seams, paper piecing, and machine appliqué.

Several of the quilts require the use of templates or special rulers. In each case, a template has been provided along with information about commercial rulers and templates available in the marketplace. You have permission to photocopy the templates and paper-piecing patterns for your personal use.

Unlike the quilts in the first book, which were all machine pieced, several in this book were hand pieced, and two examples were hand quilted. Grandmother's Flower Garden is hand pieced, and directions are provided for this technique. Several of the quilts were machine quilted on commercial sewing machines, but for the most part, they were machine quilted on long-arm quilting machines by someone other than the quiltmaker.

What's inside?

More Quilts from The Quiltmaker's Gift provides everything you need for the successful construction of nineteen different quilts. Also included are historical background on the quilt blocks, step-by-step cutting and piecing instructions with color-coded, easy-to-read diagrams, tips and techniques, as well as suggestions for creative adaptations. A special feature is the Artist's Secrets. Gail de Marcken, illustrator of *The Quiltmaker's Gift* shares her thoughts on how and why she chose each quilt pattern for the children's book. Several quilts in this book use fabric designed using Gail's illustrations from *The Quiltmaker's Gift*.

Don't miss the unusual reference features: visual glossaries inside the front and back covers, mini-lessons in every pattern, suggested print resources, and information about ongoing Quiltmaker's Gift Generosity Projects. Check the Web site (QuiltmakersGift.com) periodically for announcements of contests, challenges, and projects featuring patterns from this book.

Meet our generous quiltmakers

Quilts from The Quiltmaker's Gift and *More Quilts from The Quiltmaker's Gift* were created to celebrate the creative and philanthropic efforts of the millions of quilters worldwide who quilt just for the joy of making something useful and beautiful to give away. That being said, a few of the quiltmakers and machine quilters featured in this book are having a major impact on the national quilting scene by winning awards, writing patterns, and designing quilting fabric. Their accomplishments are noted throughout the book.

More Quilts from The Quiltmaker's Gift includes two first-time quilts made by children. Their mother and/or grandmother mentored the children. Both of these patterns are very easy for children or beginning quilters. The book also features three group quilts—one made by members of a quilt guild, one made by fabric store employees and the final one made by a group of women, some of whom have met together for over twenty-five years. Two of the quilts have been donated as raffle quilts to raise money for a school project and a charitable organization.

Sharing—in a word, that's the essential joy of quilting. This sense of sharing inspired quiltmakers throughout our region to help with several projects related to all three books. They made mini-quilts to match the book illustrations, tested patterns, and created contemporary interpretations of forgotten historical quilt blocks. The mini-quilts and the quilts made for *Quilts from The Quiltmaker's Gift* have been shown in quilt shows, fabric stores, and exhibitions all over the country.

My challenge to you

Cherish the gift of quiltmaking and continue to pass on the tradition. I recently shared my expertise with a group of young Girl Scouts who wanted to learn to quilt. They made a quilt using the Friendship Star pattern from *Quilts from The Quiltmaker's Gift* and then donated it to the Bethany Crisis Nursery.

Join forces with a friend or your quilt guild to create a generosity project in your community. The projects in this book and in *Quilts from The Quiltmaker's Gift* make a perfect starting point. All the patterns in the book include lots of diagrams and pictures to make the learning process as easy as possible.

How to Use This Book

Brackman/BlockBase Number
All blocks in this book were chosen from Barbara Brackman's *Encyclopedia of Pieced Quilt Patterns*, which catalogs blocks based on the construction type, date and source of first publication, alternate names, and similar blocks. This same number is used by Electric Quilt's BlockBase computer program which will print out templates for the block pieces at various sizes.

Meet the Quiltmaker
Wherever a butterfly appears in the text, expect some interesting description of the quiltmaker whose creative efforts are pictured nearby.

Quilt Information Chart
Look here to find important details for three quilts in three different sizes: dimensions with and before adding borders, block size, number of blocks needed and their layout, and a diagram for cutting the backing fabric for that size.

Fabric Requirement Chart
Lists fabric by fabric, piece by piece, how much fabric is needed for the different size quilts. Measurements assume 42" fabric that has been prewashed. Calculations allow for shrinkage and the trimming of selvages before measuring and cutting. For each fabric, 6" extra fabric is included as allowance for uneven yardage and/or cutting errors.

Quilt Diagram
Shows block layout and borders for three quilt sizes.

More Quilts
Many patterns feature additional quilts on this spread, along with a caption about its makers.

Block Diagrams
Show the quilt block components with pieces color-coded and alpha-labeled to coordinate with the fabric requirements and cutting charts, and to match the step-by-step block construction instructions that follow. The Brackman/BlockBase number is below the diagram.

The Quiltmaker Says
Each pattern begins with a gentle reminder of essentials for success from the Quiltmaker.

Tip Diagrams
Especially for beginners, tip diagrams expand the step-by-step instructions to show positioning of units during construction and highlight tricky spots.

Watch for the helpful bird who offers reminders of good techniques or potential hazards.

Block Construction and History Narrative
This column focuses on interesting aspects of the pattern, including historical settings and colorings, significant elements of the block construction, and adaptations and interpretations of the pattern by contemporary quiltmakers. Look for the special challenges presented by this block's construction.

Block Illustration
Gail de Marcken's illustrations of the quilt pattern in *The Quiltmaker's Gift* provide a springboard for your inspiration.

Artist's Secrets
Illustrator Gail de Marcken reveals some of the intriguing stories behind her choice of nineteenth and early twentieth century quilt patterns included in *The Quiltmaker's Gift*.

Quiltmaker's Design Challenges
For beginners and experts alike, this column offers stimulating ideas for fabric choices, plus suggestions for borders, quilt design, and settings.

Story Excerpt
Text from *The Quiltmaker's Gift* by Jeff Brumbeau graces every opening page spread.

Cutting Instructions Chart
Fabric-by-fabric, piece-by-piece instructions for cutting and crosscutting strips into shapes needed to construct the block. Number of strips and number of final pieces needed are noted for worry-free cutting.

More Features
This spread may also include step-by-step photo sequences, tidbits of interest, or additional sample quilts with stories of their makers.

Quilt Assembly
This section gives instructions for setting the finished blocks in a pleasing arrangement and sewing them together. For some patterns, diagrams show challenging assembly techniques and give advice for special settings that go well with specific blocks.

Finishing the Quilt
Outlines the final steps of quiltmaking with references to more in-depth instructions.

Meet the Quiltmakers
Look for photo collages showing the stories of novice and experienced quilters like you joining forces to make beautiful quilts.

Step-by-Step Piecing Instructions
Written instructions explain and color-coded diagrams show every step of the block construction process. Watch pressing arrows carefully. If seams are pressed in the direction indicated, intersecting seams will nest together nicely, and the final block should be nice and flat.

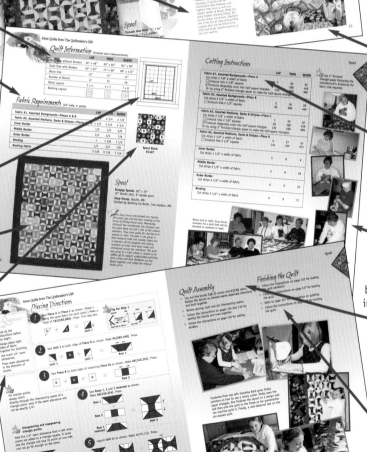

End of the Day

Serenity Now, 62" x 74"
12" blocks (20), 3 mitered borders

Joanne Larsen Line, Duluth, MN
quilted by Pam Schaefer, Moose Lake, MN

End of the Day

Brackman/BlockBase Number: 1287
Earliest publication date: unknown
Alternate names: Whirligig for Your Child

The *Farm Journal* first published the End of the Day pattern. The *Farm Journal* was established in March of 1877, and in the twentieth century they offered mail-order quilting patterns and booklets. The Kansas City Star Patterns later published the pattern as Whirligig for Your Child. The Kansas City Star Patterns were available from 1928 to 1960, and recently a book has been published with many of the patterns included.

This pattern falls under the four-patch category with sixteen squares. This interesting adaptation of a very easy block offers beginners an opportunity to play with different fabrics in designing the quilt and offers lots of practice with stitching and butting seams together. Our pattern has been updated and would be a good pattern in which to use triangle paper to make the half-square triangles.

Joanne used fabric over-dyed by artist Wendy Richardson of Brooklyn Park, MN. Pam's quilting design enhanced the feeling of peace and tranquility at the end of a busy day.

Artist's Secrets

Ah, this was one of my favorite finds when searching for quilt blocks whose names would help tell the story. Even the Quiltmaker becomes tired and must rest at the End of the Day. At the end of the story we see her resting in the gift the king gave her, surrounded by everything she values and loves.

Quiltmaker's Design Challenges

◆ Experiment with fabrics and placements so your block makes a sunset design.

◆ Reverse dark and light color placements.

◆ Use a design wall to test setting options.

◆ In keeping with the mood of the End of the Day, use a color schemes such as orange/red-orange.

◆ Make a pieced border using elements from the block, such as half-square triangles.

◆ Feed sacks and reproduction prints would give this quilt an interesting look.

◆ Try a two-color scheme to give your quilt a jazzy, funky look.

Quilt Information (finished size measurements)

	LAP	TWIN	QUEEN
Quilt Size without Borders	36" x 48"	48" x 60"	84" x 96"
Quilt Size with Borders	50" x 62"	62" x 74"	98" x 110"
Finished Block Size	12"	12"	12"
Number of Blocks	12	20	56
Block Layout	3 x 4	4 x 5	7 x 8
Backing Layout			

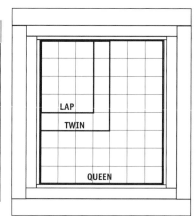

Fabric Requirements (42" wide, in yards)

	LAP	TWIN	QUEEN
Fabric #1, Light—Piece A	5/8	3/4	1 5/8
Fabric #2, Focus—Piece B	5/8	3/4	1 5/8
Fabric #3, Medium—Pieces C & D	1	1 3/8	3 1/2
Fabric #4, Dark—Pieces E & F	1	1 3/8	3 1/2
Inner Border	1/3	1/2	5/8
Middle Border	1/2	5/8	3/4
Outer Border	7/8	1 1/4	1 1/2
Binding	3/8	5/8	3/4
Backing Fabric	3 1/8	5 7/8	7 1/2

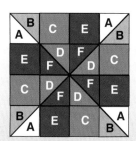

End of the Day Block
#1287

End of the Day

Day Breaker, 50" x 62"
12" blocks (12), 3 plain borders
Lynne Chilberg, Duluth, MN
quilted by Cindy Provencher, Duluth, MN

Dentist Lynne Chilberg has always been adventurous in her choice of color and design. Check out those abstract chickens in the border and the numerous black-and-white prints in the blocks. Cindy used free-motion quilting to augment the quilting pattern.

Cutting Instructions

	LAP	TWIN	QUEEN
Fabric #1, Light—Piece A			
Cut strips 3 7/8" x width of fabric	3	4	12
☐ Crosscut into 3 7/8" squares	24	40	112
☑ Crosscut diagonally once into half-square triangles	48	80	224
Or try using 3" finished triangle paper to make the half-square triangles			
Fabric #2, Focus—Piece B			
Cut strips 3 7/8" x width of fabric	3	4	12
☐ Crosscut into 3 7/8" squares	24	40	112
☑ Crosscut diagonally once into half-square triangles	48	80	224
Or try using 3" finished triangle paper to make the half-square triangles			
Fabric #3, Medium—Piece C			
Cut strips 3 1/2" x width of fabric	4	7	19
☐ Crosscut into 3 1/2" squares	48	80	224
Fabric #3, Medium—Piece D			
Cut strips 3 7/8" x width of fabric	3	4	12
☐ Crosscut into 3 7/8" squares	24	40	112
☑ Crosscut diagonally once into half-square triangles	48	80	224
Or try using 3" finished triangle paper to make the half-square triangles			
Fabric #4, Dark—Piece E			
Cut strips 3 1/2" x width of fabric	4	7	19
☐ Crosscut into 3 1/2" squares	48	80	224
Fabric #4, Dark—Piece F			
Cut strips 3 7/8" x width of fabric	3	4	12
☐ Crosscut into 3 7/8" squares	24	40	112
☑ Crosscut diagonally once into half-square triangles	48	80	224
Or try using 3" finished triangle paper to make the half-square triangles			
Inner Border			
Cut strips 1 1/2" x width of fabric	5	8	10
Middle Border			
Cut strips 2 1/2" x width of fabric	5	8	10
Outer Border			
Cut strips 4 1/2" x width of fabric	6	9	10
Binding			
Cut strips 2 1/4" x width of fabric	6	9	11

For blocks like End of the Day, make a color key and keep it handy for reference while cutting and piecing.

Cutting triangles made with triangle paper.

Chain piecing for mass production.

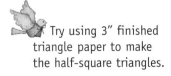

Try using 3" finished triangle paper to make the half-square triangles.

Auditioning borders.

Scrap organization for End of the Day.

Spool

Threads that Bind, 51" x 64"
12" blocks (12), 3 borders

Shelly McKeever, Makinen, MN
& Barbara McKeever, Duluth, MN
quilted by Barbara McKeever

Spool

Artist's Secrets

I was delighted to find Spool for the picture in which the Quiltmaker sews. I really like simple patterns like this one. My favorite quilts to make are easy squares using wonderful fabrics. In searching for names for quilt patterns, I was surprised how few had anything to do with sewing. There are many stars but no needles and thread.

Brackman/BlockBase Number: 1807a
Earliest publication date: 1906
Alternate names: Fred's Spool, Spool and Spool Quilt

The Spool pattern is a perennial favorite of quiltmakers. First published in 1906 in *Practical Needlework: Quilt Patterns* by C. W. Calkins & Co., of Boston, MA, the pattern was designed by Clara Stone. This booklet was one of a series on needlework. Stone had contributed patterns to *Hearth and Home,* and this booklet included many published in the magazine. This pattern adaptation was originally written by Alice Gammel in Polly Prindle's *Book of American Patchwork Quilts.* Grossett & Dunlop, New York, 1973. Reprinted by Dover Publications.

The Spool pattern falls in the category of nine-patch designs. The spool quilt is a perfect pattern to use with scraps because no piece is larger than a 2 7/8" square. Triangle paper was used to create the many half-square triangle pieces but directions are also given for those who choose not to use this method. The use of triangle paper makes the quilt's construction easy for a child or a beginning quilter. Ten-year-old Shelly found it easy, fast, and fun to use the paper. She thought it was like eating popcorn, once you start it's hard to stop.

Quiltmaker's Design Challenges

◆ Select a theme fabric and coordinate the triangles. Shelly's grandmother threw in a couple squares of fabric with monkey faces on them. See if you can find the three monkeys hiding among the wild fabrics.

◆ Try to make each spool different. The quilt done by the Soup Group was put together this way. The only constraint placed on the group was that light fabrics be used for the background pieces.

◆ Combine plaids, homespun, and calico prints for an old-fashioned look.

◆ Use stripe fabrics for the body of the spool block.

◆ Try a monochromatic color scheme, such as multiple shades of blue.

◆ For an Amish look, use bright solid colors with black for the background pieces.

◆ Use sashing strips between the blocks to set off the spools.

◆ Make a pieced border of the individual spools, placing one spool horizontally and the next vertically.

This is a first quilt for Shelly McKeever, age ten. She spent several Saturdays in Duluth with her Grandmother Barb McKeever, and together they came up with this colorful version of Spools. Shelly has many hobbies including fishing, Girl Scouts, dance, and archery. Hopefully this is the first of many joint quilting projects. Barb did the stitch-in-the-ditch and border machine quilting on her Juki machine.

Some said there was magic in her fingers. Some whispered that her needles and cloth were gifts of the bewitched.

Quilt Information (finished size measurements)

	LAP	TWIN	QUEEN
Quilt Size without Borders	36" x 48"	60" x 84"	84" x 96"
Quilt Size with Borders	50" x 62"	74" x 98"	98" x 110"
Block Size	12"	12"	12"
Number of Blocks	12	35	56
Block Layout	3 x 4	5 x 7	7 x 8
Backing Layout			

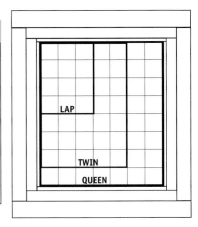

Fabric Requirements (42" wide, in yards)

	LAP	TWIN	QUEEN
Fabric #1, Assorted Backgrounds—Pieces A & B	1 1/4	3 1/4	4 7/8
Fabric #2, Assorted Mediums, Darks & Stripes—Pieces C & D	1 1/2	3 3/4	5 3/4
Inner Border	1/3	1/2	5/8
Middle Border	1/2	3/4	7/8
Outer Border	1	1 3/8	1 1/2
Binding	1/2	2/3	7/8
Backing Fabric	3 1/8	5 7/8	7 1/4

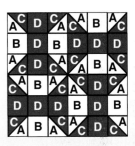

**Spool Block
#1407**

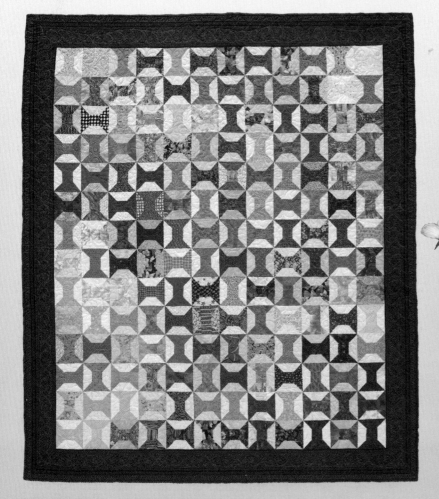

Spool

Scrappy Spools, 62" x 72"
12" blocks (42), 6" border print

Soup Group, Duluth, MN
quilted by Quilting Up North, Two Harbors, MN

The Soup Group was formed over twenty-five years ago and has been meeting at the home of Shirley Kirsch every Wednesday. Although the membership has changed over the years, there are still a few of the original members. They make quilts for charities and anyone in need. The joke in the group is that everyone talks and nobody listens, but in between all the laughter and talking, hundreds of quilts have been made and distributed across the northland. This quilt was given to a high school in Duluth to be raffled off to support underfunded activities. Jane Carnes and Barb McKeever put the blocks together and added the mitered border print.

Cutting Instructions

	LAP	TWIN	QUEEN
Fabric #1, Assorted Backgrounds—Piece A			
Cut strips 2 7/8" x width of fabric	7	20	32
☐ Crosscut into 2 7/8" squares	96	280	448
☒ Crosscut diagonally once into half square triangles	192	560	896
Or try using 2" finished triangle paper to make the half-square triangles			
Fabric #1, Assorted Backgrounds—Piece B			
Cut strips 2 1/2" x width of fabric	6	18	28
☐ Crosscut into 2 1/2" squares	96	280	448
Fabric #2, Assorted Mediums, Darks & Stripes—Piece C			
Cut strips 2 7/8" x width of fabric	7	20	32
☐ Crosscut into 2 7/8" squares	96	280	448
☒ Crosscut diagonally once into half square triangles	192	560	896
Or try using 2" finished triangle paper to make the half-square triangles			
Fabric #2, Assorted Mediums, Darks & Stripes—Piece D			
Cut strips 2 1/2" x width of fabric	9	27	42
☐ Crosscut into 2 1/2" squares	144	420	672
Inner Border			
Cut strips 1 1/2" x width of fabric	5	8	9
Middle Border			
Cut strips 2 1/2" x width of fabric	5	8	10
Outer Border			
Cut strips 4 1/2" x width of fabric	6	9	10
Binding			
Cut strips 2 1/4" x width of fabric	6	9	11

Use 2" finished triangle paper following the manufacturer's directions for fabric size required.

Below and at right: Soup Group members tie quilts that will be donated to someone in need.

The Soup Group in action—from the top: Ferne Liberty works on a binding, Vicki Fosnacht plans her next shopping trip while someone gets out the soup bowls, Carol Jean Brooks hand sews a binding, Betty Firth does some unsewing, Joanne Line cuts strips for 9-patch.

17

Piecing Directions

The Quiltmaker says . . .

Read all the instructions before you begin.

Always place right sides of fabric together for stitching.

Use scant 1/4" seam allowances.

Press seam allowances in the direction of arrows.

For precise points, always stitch directly through the intersecting seams of a triangle point, even if the seam allowance will not be exactly 1/4".

Disappearing and reappearing triangle points

Note the 1/4" seam allowance that is left when pieces are added to a triangle square. It looks like the triangle will lose its point on one side and not go far enough on the other.

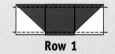

Row 1

As the rows are stitched together, the seam allowance disappears, and sharp triangle points will reappear when you stitch through the intersecting seams.

The finished block will also have this extra seam allowance on all sides. The star points should end 1/4" before the edge to allow for the block-joining seam.

When you sew the block together, stitching exactly through the intersecting seams of the star points, the excess will disappear, and perfect star points will reappear.

1 Sew **Piece A** to **Piece C** as shown. (Make 4 using the same fabric for each spool.) Make a total of **192(560,896)**. Press. Trim dog ears.

Unit 1

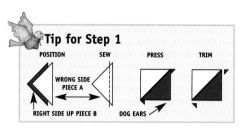

Tip for Step 1

2 Sew **Unit 1** to both sides of **Piece D** as shown. Make **96(280,448)**. Press.

Unit 1   Unit 1   Row 1

3 Sew **Piece B** to both sides of remaining **Piece D**s as shown. Make **48(140,224)**. Press.

B + D + B =

Row 2

4 Sew **Rows 1, 2** and **1 reversed** as shown. Make **48(140,224)**. Press.

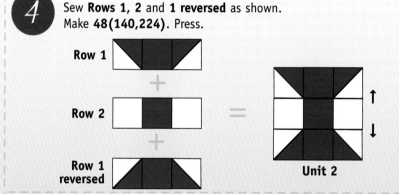

Row 1
+
Row 2
+
Row 1 reversed
=
Unit 2

5 Layout **Unit 2**s as shown. Make **24(70,112)**. Press.

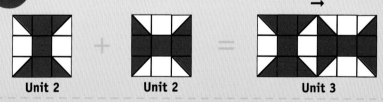

Unit 2   Unit 2   Unit 3

6 Sew two **Unit 3**s together as shown. Make **12(35,56)**. Press.

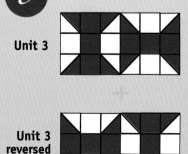

Unit 3

Unit 3 reversed

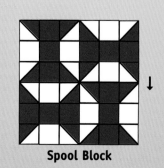

Spool Block

Quilt Assembly

◆ Lay out the blocks **3(5,7)** across and **4(7,8)** down. Rotate the blocks so pressed seams alternate directions and butt together.

◆ Before sewing, butt and pin intersecting seams.

◆ Follow the instructions on pages 134 and 135 for sewing the blocks and rows together.

◆ Follow the instructions on page 136 for adding borders.

Finishing the Quilt

◆ Follow the instructions on page 137 for making the quilt sandwich.

◆ Follow the instructions on page 137 for basting the quilt.

◆ Refer to page 137 for information on quilting.

◆ Follow the instructions on page 138 for binding the quilt.

Clockwise from top left: Grandma Barb gives Shelly pointers on how to use a rotary cutter. Shelly sews the paper triangles. She finalizes the layout on a design wall and then pins the quilt to the frame so her grandmother can machine quilt it. Finally, a well-deserved rest on the pin-basted quilt.

Next-Door Neighbor

Rainbow Coalition, 62" x 87"
12" blocks (24), 2 plain borders

Nancy Loving Tubesing, Pacitas, NM
quilted by Pam Schaefer, Moose Lake, MN

Next-Door Neighbor

Artist's Secrets

I have lived in many countries and believe we should treat all people as next-door neighbors. This pattern is placed near the Trip Around the World to emphasize that idea.

Next-Door Neighbor

Brackman/BlockBase Number: 2787

Earliest publication date: 1910 (Practical Needlework)

Alternate name: Square Up, Star of Beauty, July Fourth, Patriotic Quilt

The first reference to Next-Door Neighbor is in *Practical Needlework* in 1910. The Ladies' Art Company also listed the pattern in their 1922 catalog as pattern #465. Originally the pattern was done in red, white, and blues and was viewed as a patriotic quilt. With the tragic events of September 11, 2001, we are seeing more quilts done in this color scheme.

Next-Door Neighbor is a relatively easy quilt to make and lends itself to many interesting interpretations. This book provides you with four samples, and each one looks different because of the colorations used.

Quiltmaker's Design Challenges

◆ Try making a monochromatic color scheme.

◆ Set the blocks on point and add sashing and cornerstones.

◆ Straight set the blocks and add sashing and cornerstones.

◆ Try using a plain alternate block to provide open space for highlighting quilting.

◆ Make a patriotic quilt using red, white, and blues.

◆ Use reproduction fabrics to give the quilt an antique look.

"I give my quilts to those who are poor or homeless," she told all who knocked on her door. "They are not for the rich."

Nancy loves batik fabrics in vibrant colors. Her use of color makes this quilt sparkle. Pam did a beautiful job with the machine quilting, making the stars stand out from the rest of the pattern.

Quilt Information (finished size measurements)

	LAP	TWIN	QUEEN
Quilt Size without Borders	36" x 48"	48" x 72"	84" x 96"
Quilt Size with Borders	50" x 62"	62" x 86"	98" x 110"
Finished Block Size	12"	12"	12"
Number of Blocks	12	24	56
Block Layout	3 x 4	4 x 6	7 x 8
Backing Layout			

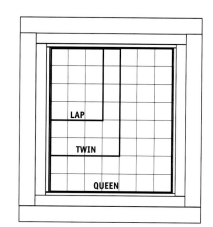

Fabric Requirements (42" wide, in yards)

	LAP	TWIN	QUEEN
Fabric #1, Focus—Piece A	5/8	1	2 1/4
Fabric #2, 1st Light—Piece B	1/2	3/4	1 5/8
Fabric #3, 2nd Light—Piece C	7/8	1 1/4	2 2/3
Fabric #4, 1st Medium—Piece D	1/2	1/2	7/8
Fabric #5, 2nd Medium—Piece E	5/8	1	2 1/4
Fabric #6, Dark—Piece F	1/2	1/2	7/8
Inner Border	1/3	1/2	5/8
Middle Border	1/2	3/4	7/8
Outer Border	1	1 3/8	1 1/2
Binding	1/2	2/3	7/8
Backing Fabric	3 1/8	5 7/8	7 1/8

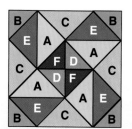

**Next-Door Neighbor Block
#2787**

Next-Door Neighbor

Awesome Neighborhood, 54" x 79"
12" blocks (12), 2 plain borders and
1 checkerboard border

Barbara McKeever, Duluth, MN
quilted by Quilting Up North, Two Harbors, MN

*Barb enjoyed testing patterns for this book
and is always willing to give Joanne a hand with
any project. Merry and Rosemary, of Quilting
Up North, did an overall quilting design
to enhance the pattern.*

Cutting Instructions

	LAP	TWIN	QUEEN
Fabric #1, Focus—Piece A			
Cut strips 5 1/8" x width of fabric	3	6	14
☐ Crosscut into 5 1/8" squares	24	48	112
◩ Crosscut diagonally once into half-square triangles	48	96	224
Fabric #2, 1st Light—Piece B			
Cut strips 3 7/8" x width of fabric	3	5	12
☐ Crosscut into 3 7/8" squares	24	48	112
◩ Crosscut diagonally once into half-square triangles	48	96	224
Fabric #3, 2nd Light—Piece C			
Cut strips 7 1/4" x width of fabric	3	5	12
☐ Crosscut into 7 1/4" squares	12	24	56
⊠ Crosscut diagonally twice into quarter-square triangles	48	96	224
Fabric #4, 1st Medium—Piece D			
Cut strips 3 7/8" x width of fabric	2	3	6
☐ Crosscut into 3 7/8" squares	12	24	56
◩ Crosscut diagonally once into half-square triangles	24	48	112
Fabric #5, 2nd Medium—Piece E			
Cut strips 5 1/8" x width of fabric	3	6	14
☐ Crosscut into 5 1/8" squares	24	48	112
◩ Crosscut diagonally once into half-square triangles	48	96	224
Fabric #6, Dark—Piece F			
Cut strips 3 7/8" x width of fabric	2	3	6
☐ Crosscut into 3 7/8" squares	12	24	56
◩ Crosscut diagonally once into half-square triangles	24	48	112
Inner Border			
Cut strips 1 1/2" x width of fabric	5	8	9
Middle Border			
Cut strips 2 1/2" x width of fabric	5	8	10
Outer Border			
Cut strips 4 1/2" x width of fabric	6	9	10
Binding			
Cut strips 2 1/4" x width of fabric	6	9	11

For blocks like Next-Door Neighbor, make a color key and keep it handy for reference while cutting and piecing.

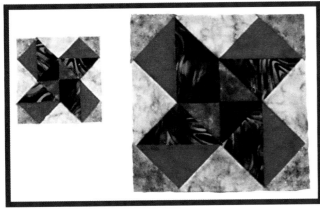

Fabric scanned into a computer program gives the quilter a realistic look at what the final block will look like.

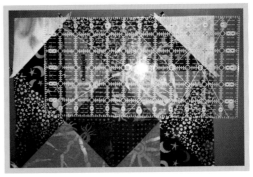

Squaring up the block.

Piecing Directions

1 Sew **Piece A** to **Piece E** as shown. Make **48(96,224)**. Press. Trim dog-ears.

2 Sew **Piece D** to **Piece F** as shown. Make **24(48,112)**. Press. Trim dog-ears.

3 Sew two **Unit 2**s together as shown. Make **12(24,56)**. Press. Trim dog-ears.

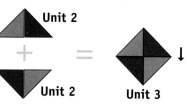

4 Sew 24(48,112) **Unit 1**s to opposite sides of **Unit 3** as shown. Make **12(24,56)**. Press. Trim dog-ears.

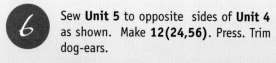

5 Sew **Piece C** to opposite sides of remaining **Unit 1**s as shown. Make **24(48,112)**. Press. Trim dog-ears.

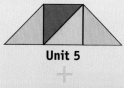

6 Sew **Unit 5** to opposite sides of **Unit 4** as shown. Make **12(24,56)**. Press. Trim dog-ears.

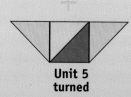

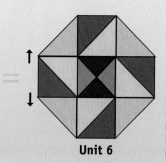
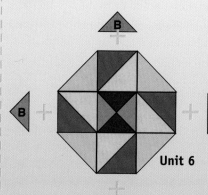

7 Sew **Piece B** to the four corners of **Unit 6** as shown. Make **12(24,56)**. Press. Trim dog-ears.

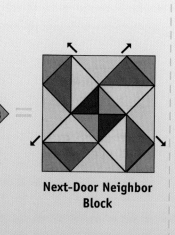

Next-Door Neighbor Block

Quilt Assembly

◇ Lay out the blocks **3(4,7)** across and **4(6,8)** down. Rotate the blocks so pressed seams alternate directions and butt together.

◇ Before sewing, butt and pin intersecting seams.

◇ Follow the instructions on pages 134–135 for sewing the blocks and rows together.

◇ Follow the instructions on page 136 for adding borders.

Finishing the Quilt

◇ Follow the instructions on page 137 for making the quilt sandwich.

◇ Follow the instructions on page 137 for basting the quilt.

◇ Refer to page 137 for information on quilting.

◇ Follow the instructions on page 138 for binding the quilt.

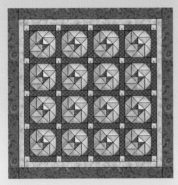

Dee Wojciehowski's computer-aided quilt designs, made with BlockBase and Electric Quilt 5 show a wide variety of layouts possible with the Next-Door Neighbor pattern.

Next-Door Neighbor

Charity Begins at Home
50" x 62", 12" blocks (12),
3 plain borders

Joanne Larsen Line,
Duluth, MN
quilted by Jan Seidel,
Herbster, WI

Joanne chose some old-fashioned fabric to try to make the two different star patterns stand out. Jan did an overall quilting pattern that enhanced the pattern design.

Next-Door Neighbor

Neighborhood Blues, 62" x 76"
12" blocks (24), 2 plain borders and 1 stripe border

Nancy Loving Tubesing, Placitas, NM
quilted by Sue Munns, Duluth, MN

Nancy chose a monochromatic color theme to make Neighborhood Blues. Sue has been doing long-arm quilting for several years now and did freehand quilting to enhance the quilt blocks.

Carol Jean works on Nancy's binding.

Peace & Plenty

Peaceful Easy Feeling, 62"x 74"
12" blocks (20), 2 plain borders
and 1 checkerboard border

Joanne Larsen Line, Duluth, MN
quilted by Sue Munns, Duluth, MN

Peace & Plenty

Peace & Plenty

Brackman/BlockBase Number: 1201

Earliest publication date: unknown

Alternate names: None given

The first recorded mention of the Peace & Plenty block occurs in the *Farm Journal*. The *Farm Journal* was a periodical established in March of 1877. In the twentieth century they offered mail-order patterns and booklets. Over time they absorbed other periodicals of the day such as *Country Gentlemen*, *The Farmer's Wife,* and *Household Journal*. Some of their patterns were reproduced in Rachel Martin's *Modern Patchwork*, published by Country Side Press of Philadelphia in 1970.

Originally the Peace & Plenty block was done as a 2-color quilt using colors such as blue and white to make a dramatic statement. The examples in this book use several colors and are also very dramatic looking. This pattern introduces quarter-square triangles thus eliminating bulky seam intersections.

Quiltmaker's Design Challenges

◆ Try making a two-color quilt for a dramatic look.

◆ Consider making a flannel quilt for a warm and peaceful feeling.

◆ Try using holiday fabrics or novelty prints.

◆ Amish colors would be stunning in this quilt.

◆ Set the blocks on point and use setting triangles to give a totally different look.

◆ Try using sashing and cornerstones to separate the blocks.

Joanne used planned scraps and an over-dyed 100 percent cotton fabric by fiber artist Wendy Richardson for the border and several of the block pieces. Sue did freehand quilting in the body of the quilt and outlined the flowers in the border.

"I may look poor, but in truth my heart is full to bursting, filled with memories of all the happiness I've given and received. I'm the richest man I know."

27

Quilt Information (finished size measurements)

	LAP	TWIN	QUEEN
Quilt Size without Borders	48" x 60"	60" x 84"	84" x 96"
Quilt Size with Borders	62" x 74"	74" x 98"	98" x 110"
Finished Block Size	12"	12"	12"
Number of Blocks	20	35	56
Block Layout	4 x 5	5 x 7	7 x 8
Backing Layout			

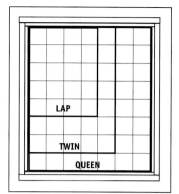

Fabric Requirements (42" wide, in yards)

	LAP	TWIN	QUEEN
Fabric #1, Light—Piece A & B	2	3 1/4	5 1/4
Fabric #2, Assorted Mediums—Piece C	1	1 5/8	2 5/8
Fabric #3, Assorted Darks—Piece D	1 1/8	1 3/4	2 3/4
Inner Border	1/3	1/2	5/8
Middle Border	1/2	3/4	7/8
Outer Border	1	1 3/8	1 1/2
Binding	1/2	2/3	7/8
Backing Fabric	3 1/8	5 7/8	7 1/4

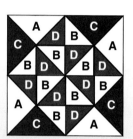

**Peace & Plenty Block
#1201**

Peace & Plenty

Peace & Plenty Squared, 48" x 60"
12" blocks (12), 1 border print

Nancy Loving Tubesing, Placitas, NM
quilted by the Tami Bradley, Henderson, NV

Nancy, who was the co-author of Quilts from
The Quiltmaker's Gift, *used* The Quiltmaker's Gift
*fabric line designed by Benartex. The machine
quilting done by Tami enhances this beautiful
rendition of Peace & Plenty.*

Cutting Instructions

	LAP	TWIN	QUEEN
Fabric #1, Light—Piece A			
Cut strips 7 1/4" x width of fabric	4	7	12
☐ Crosscut into 7 1/4" squares	20	35	56
☒ Crosscut diagonally twice into quarter-square triangles	80	140	224
Fabric #1, Light—Piece B			
Cut strips 3 7/8" x width of fabric	8	14	23
☐ Crosscut into 3 7/8" squares	80	140	224
◲ Crosscut diagonally once into half-square triangles	160	280	448
Fabric #2, Assorted Mediums—Piece C			
Cut strips 7 1/4" x width of fabric	4	7	12
☐ Crosscut into 7 1/4" squares	20	35	56
☒ Crosscut diagonally twice into quarter-square triangles	80	140	224
Fabric #3, Assorted Darks—Piece D			
Cut strips 3 7/8" x width of fabric	8	14	23
☐ Crosscut into 3 7/8" squares	80	140	224
◲ Crosscut diagonally once into half-square triangles	160	280	448
Inner Border			
Cut strips 1 1/2" x width of fabric	6	8	9
Middle Border			
Cut strips 2 1/2" x width of fabric	6	8	10
Outer Border			
Cut strips 4 1/2" x width of fabric	7	9	10
Binding			
Cut strips 2 1/4" x width of fabric	7	9	11

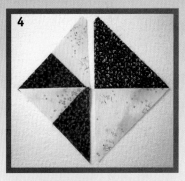

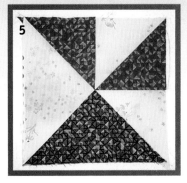

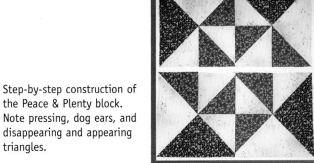

For blocks like Peace & Plenty, make a color key and keep it handy for reference while cutting and piecing.

Step-by-step construction of the Peace & Plenty block. Note pressing, dog ears, and disappearing and appearing triangles.

Carol Jean finishes the binding on Nancy's Peace & Plenty quilt.

Piecing Directions

Read all the instructions before you begin.

Always place right sides of fabric together for stitching.

Use scant 1/4" seam allowances.

Press seam allowances in the direction of arrows.

For precise points, always stitch directly through the intersecting seams of a triangle point, even if the seam allowance will not be exactly 1/4".

1 Sew **Piece C** to **Piece A**. Make **80(140,224)**. Press. Trim dog-ears.

Unit 1

2 Sew **Piece B** to **Piece D**. Make **160(280,448)**. Press. Trim dog-ears.

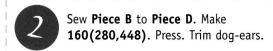
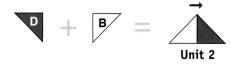

Unit 2

3 Sew **Unit 2**s together as shown. Make **80(140,224)**. Press. Trim dog-ears.

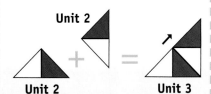

Unit 2   **Unit 2**   **Unit 3**

4 Sew **Unit 1** to **Unit 3**. Make **80(140,224)**. Press **40(70,112)** toward **Unit 1** and **40(70,112)** toward **Unit 3**. Trim dog-ears.

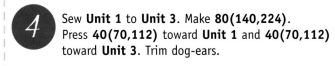
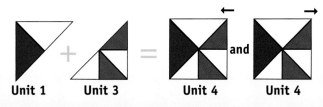

Unit 1   **Unit 3**   **Unit 4**   and   **Unit 4**

5 Sew **Unit 4**s together as shown. Make **40(70,112)**. Press. Trim dog-ears.

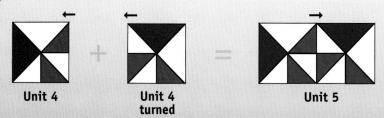

Unit 4   **Unit 4 turned**   **Unit 5**

6 Sew **Unit 5**s together as shown. Make **20(35,56)**. Press.

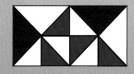
Unit 5

Unit 5 turned

Peace & Plenty Block

Peace & Plenty

Peace on Earth, 46" x 58"
12" blocks (12), 2 plain borders

Andy Lien, Superior, WI
quilted by Cindy Provencher, Duluth, MN

Andy, who is a former owner of a quilt shop, loves to work with color. For this quilt, she used holiday fabrics. She enjoys sharing her quilting skills with others. Andy is also a master gardener. Cindy has her own long-arm machine quilting business and enjoys working with quilters to enhance their quilts.

Peace & Plenty

Sampler Peace & Plenty, 46" x 58"
12" blocks (12), 2 plain borders

Joanne Larsen Line, Duluth, MN
quilted by Sue Munns, Duluth, MN

Joanne set 6" finished blocks inside the 12" finished Peace & Plenty blocks. The quilt features the Benartex fabric line from The Quiltmaker's Gift.

Quilt Assembly

◆ Lay out the blocks **4(5,7)** across and **5(7,8)** down. Rotate the blocks so pressed seams alternate directions and butt together.

◆ Before sewing, butt and pin intersecting seams.

◆ Follow the instructions on pages 134 and 135 for sewing the blocks and rows together.

◆ Follow the instructions on page 136 for adding borders. Make checkerboard border from leftover scraps.

Finishing the Quilt

◆ Follow the instructions on page 137 for making the quilt sandwich.

◆ Follow the instructions on page 137 for basting the quilt.

◆ Refer to page 137 for information on quilting.

◆ Follow the instructions on page 138 for binding the quilt.

Windblown Square

Falling Leaves, 50" x 62"
12" blocks (12), 3 plain borders

Joanne Larsen Line, Duluth, MN
quilted by Karen McTavish, Duluth, MN

Windblown Square

Artist's Secrets

This was another neat match. The "square" is blown out the window and away from the King. I hope you all noticed it came to earth in northern Minnesota and was used for warmth on the sled pulled by the dogs in a snowstorm.

Windblown Square

Brackman/BlockBase Number: 2444
Earliest publication date: Late 1920s
Alternate names: Balkan Puzzle, Zigzag Tile, Whirlpools, Wind-blown Star

Windblown Square was first published by Ruby Short McKim of McKim Studios in Independence, MO. McKim Studios was a mail-order source for patterns, and Ruby wrote a syndicated newspaper column with full-size patterns during the late 1920s and 1930s. Florence LaGanke Harris, writing as Nancy Page for a syndicated mail-order column, later published the pattern as Whirlpools. The pattern Wind-blown Star was featured in the book, *Romance of the Patchwork Quilt in America*, written by Carrie A. Hall and Rose G. Kretsinger. Caxton Printers of Caldwell, ID published this book in 1935. Dover Publications, NY, in 1962, reprinted the Windblown Square pattern in the book *101 Patchwork Patterns*.

Historically this pattern was done in three colors, but we have updated the original pattern to give a more contemporary look using several coordinating fabrics along with a focus fabric and a background fabric. Mary and Marcia's quilt (page 37) has a trendy look and features Marcia's hand-dyed fabrics. Windblown Square is a square in a square in a square in a square. It is a challenge to get all the points perfect, but it is achievable by squaring up the block after each round is added. Pinning the diagonal or multiple seams exactly is the secret. Be sure to read page 133 for helpful hints on precision pinning. This is also a perfect quilt to learn a new skill—quarter-square triangles.

Joanne loves fabric with leaves and buys it all the time. In fact, she loved this fabric so much she accidentally bought it twice. Karen incorporated trapunto for three different layers of texture into the quilt design. She also did some beautiful cable stitching with trapunto in the second border. Karen is well known for her fabulous trapunto work.

Quiltmaker's Design Challenges

- Use a novelty leaf fabric to give the feeling of wind-blown leaves.

- Consider a variety of color schemes. What about an analogous color scheme, earth tones, sea and sky, or harvest colors, or primaries?

- This quilt works well with a scrappy look. Try using many different background fabrics.

- Show off juvenile prints or novelty fabrics in the center squares.

- Create a pieced border using one or more elements from the Windblown Square block.

A cold, fierce wind was blowing and it did not look like the poor bird would make it to shore.

33

Quilt Information (finished size measurements)

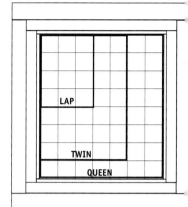

	LAP	TWIN	QUEEN
Quilt Size without Borders	36" x 48"	60" x 84"	84" x 96"
Quilt Size with Borders	50" x 62"	74" x 98"	98" x 110"
Finished Block Size	12"	12"	12"
Number of Blocks	12	35	56
Block Layout	3 x 4	5 x 7	7 x 8
Backing Layout			

Fabric Requirements (42" wide, in yards)

	LAP	TWIN	QUEEN
Fabric #1, Light—Pieces A, B & C	1 1/2	3 1/8	5
Fabric #2, Medium—Pieces D & E	1	1 7/8	2 3/4
Fabric #3, Focus—Pieces F & G	1	1 7/8	2 3/4
Inner Border	1/3	1/2	5/8
Middle Border	1/2	3/4	7/8
Outer Border	1	1 3/8	1 1/2
Binding	1/2	2/3	7/8
Backing Fabric	3 1/8	5 7/8	7 1/4

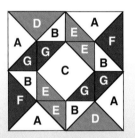

**Windblown Square Block
#2444**

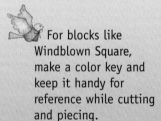

For blocks like Windblown Square, make a color key and keep it handy for reference while cutting and piecing.

Windblown Square

Autumn Leaves of Blue and Brown, 50" x 62"
12" blocks (12), 3 plain borders

Joanne Larsen Line, Duluth, MN
quilted by Janet Peterson, Solon Springs, WI

Another beautiful fabric with gorgeous leaves makes up this variation of Windblown Square. Jan Peterson is a relatively new long-arm quilter and honored her mother by naming her business after her, Toni's Daughter. Needless to say, Toni cried when she found out. Jan takes advantage of every opportunity to advance her skills.

Cutting Instructions

	LAP	TWIN	QUEEN
Fabric #1, Light—Piece A			
Cut strips 7 1/4" x width of fabric	3	7	12
☐ Crosscut into 7 1/4" squares	12	35	56
⊠ Crosscut diagonally twice into quarter-square triangles	48	140	224
Fabric #1, Light—Piece B			
Cut strips 3 7/8" x width of fabric	3	7	12
☐ Crosscut into 3 7/8" squares	24	70	112
◪ Crosscut diagonally once into half-square triangles	48	140	224
Fabric #1, Light—Piece C			
Cut strips 4 3/4" x width of fabric	2	5	7
☐ Crosscut into 4 3/4" squares	12	35	56
Fabric #2, Medium—Piece D			
Cut strips 7 1/4" x width of fabric	2	4	6
☐ Crosscut into 7 1/4" squares	6	18	28
⊠ Crosscut diagonally twice into quarter-square triangles	24	70	112
Fabric #2, Medium—Piece E			
Cut strips 3 7/8" x width of fabric	3	7	12
☐ Crosscut into 3 7/8" squares	24	70	112
◪ Crosscut diagonally once into half-square triangles	48	140	224
Fabric #3, Focus—Piece F			
Cut strips 7 1/4" x width of fabric	2	4	6
☐ Crosscut into 7 1/4" squares	6	18	28
⊠ Crosscut diagonally twice into quarter-square triangles	24	70	112
Fabric #3, Focus—Piece G			
Cut strips 3 7/8" x width of fabric	3	7	12
☐ Crosscut into 3 7/8" squares	24	70	112
◪ Crosscut diagonally once into half-square triangles	48	140	224
Inner Border			
Cut strips 1 1/2" x width of fabric	5	8	9
Middle Border			
Cut strips 2 1/2" x width of fabric	5	8	10
Outer Border			
Cut strips 4 1/2" x width of fabric	6	9	10
Binding			
Cut strips 2 1/4" x width of fabric	6	9	11

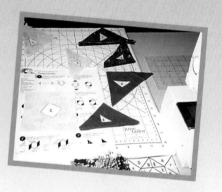

Windblown Square test blocks
from all over the country.

Piecing Directions

1 Sew **Piece E** to opposite sides of **Piece C** as shown. Make **12(35,56)**. Press. Trim dog-ears.

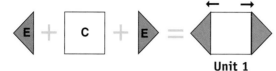

2 Sew **Piece G** to opposite sides of **Unit 1** as shown. Make **12(35,56)**. Press. Trim dog-ears.

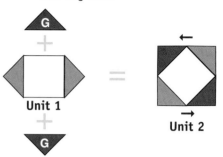

3 Sew **Piece B** to remaining **Piece E**s as shown. Make **24(70,112)**. Press. Trim dog-ears.

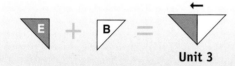

4 Sew **Unit 3** to opposite sides of **Unit 2** as shown. Make **12(35,56)**. Press. Trim dog-ears.

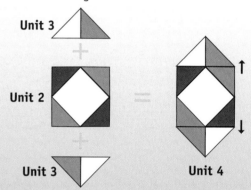

5 Sew **Piece B** to remaining **Piece G**s as shown. Make **24(70,112)**. Press. Trim dog-ears.

6 Sew **Unit 5** to opposite sides of **Unit 4** as shown. Make **12(35,56)**. Press. Trim dog-ears.

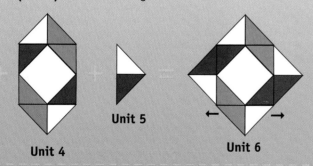

7 Sew **Piece A** to **Piece D** as shown. Make **24(70,112)**. Press. Trim dog-ears.

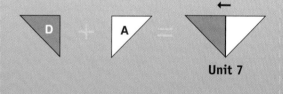

8 Sew **Unit 7** to opposite sides of **Unit 6** as shown. Make **12(35,56)**. Press. Trim dog-ears.

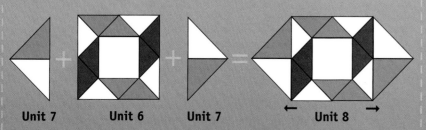

9 Sew **Piece A** to **Piece F** as shown. Make **24 (70, 112)**. Press. Trim dog-ears.

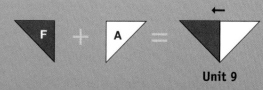

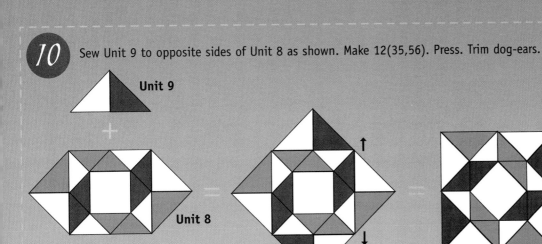

10 Sew Unit 9 to opposite sides of Unit 8 as shown. Make 12(35,56). Press. Trim dog-ears.

Unit 9

Unit 8

Unit 9

**Windblown Square
Block**

Quilt Assembly

Lay out the blocks **4(5,7)** across and **5(7,8)** down. Rotate the blocks so pressed seams alternate directions and butt together.

◆ Before sewing, butt and pin intersecting seams.

◆ Follow the instructions on pages 134 and 135 for sewing the blocks and rows together.

◆ Follow the instructions on page 136 for adding borders. Make checkerboard border from leftover scraps.

Finishing the Quilt

◆ Follow the instructions on pages 137–138 for making the quilt sandwich, basting, quilting, and binding the quilt.

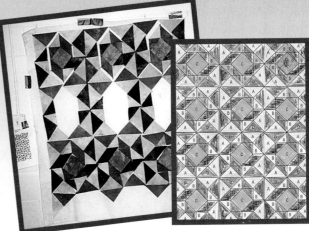

Above: Laying out the blocks in progress to match the color plan (pinned to the design wall and shown above right).

Windblown Square

Testing the Bonds of Family, 51 1/2" x 63 1/2"
12" blocks (12), 2 plain borders

Mary and Marcia Bowker, Duluth, MN
quilted by Marcia Bowker

This is Mary and Marcia's first joint project. Marcia hand dyed the fabric and used a color mockup for the design. Mary did the machine piecing and put the quilt together. Marcia did the original machine quilting using her legacy machine. In their spare time this talented mother-daughter duo make and sell crafts and clothing throughout the northland. Mary is a retired special education teacher, and Marcia is an occupational therapist, who is a certified hand therapist.

37

All Kinds

The Joy of Sharing, 50" x 62"
12" blocks (12), 3 borders

Joanne Larsen Line, Duluth, MN
quilted by Karen McTavish, Duluth, MN

All Kinds

Artist's Secrets

It takes all kinds of people to make a world and all kinds of color, patterns, and pieces to make up a quilt.

Brackman/BlockBase Number: 3072

Earliest publication date: 1898 (Ladies' Art Catalog)

Alternate names: Beggar's Block, Cats & Mice, Turnstile, and Farmers Puzzle

Crowell first published Beggar's Block in the *Household Journal* in the early twentieth century, and the pattern was sold under the name Aunt Jane. The pattern later appeared in the 1935 book *The Romance of the Patchwork Quilt in America* written by Carrie A. Hall and Rose Kretsinger. Dover Publications reprinted the book.

The pattern was also published in a Nancy Page column with the name Turnstile. This syndicated mail-order column written by Florence LaGanke Harris appeared in many periodicals in the late 1920s through the 1940s.

The pattern originally required set-in seams, but the pattern has been updated eliminating the need for them. Three interpretations of the pattern are shown including one that features hand quilting.

Quiltmaker's Design Challenges

◆ Do a stacked-brick border treatment using Piece D. Or do a sawtooth inner border of half-square triangles with an outer plain border.

◆ Feature a special fabric for Piece H. Joanne used a poinsettia fabric in The Joy of Sharing.

◆ Recreate the pattern in vintage fabrics or reproductions from your favorite era.

◆ Try a funky novelty fabric or a wild animal print for Piece D and Piece E.

◆ Use a black background with wild florals, primaries, or jewel tones for the other fabrics.

◆ Consider using flannel as backing for this or any quilt. It makes a cozy comforter.

◆ Make one extra block and use it for your label. The center of the block is perfect to record information.

When at last there was no one left in town who had not received something, the king decided to go out into the world and find others who might be in need of his gifts.

Judy Timm was willing to share a beautiful piece of poinsettia fabric and also the background fabric with Joanne so she could make this holiday version of All Kinds. Sharing ideas and fabrics is one of the many generous acts of kindness quilters do. Karen used machine trapunto to highlight areas of this quilt.

Quilt Information (finished size measurements)

	LAP	TWIN	QUEEN
Quilt Size without Borders	36" x 48"	60" x 84"	84" x 96"
Quilt Size with Borders	50" x 62"	74" x 98"	98" x 110"
Finished Block Size	12"	12"	12"
Number of Blocks	12	35	56
Block Layout	3 x 4	5 x 7	7 x 8
Backing Layout			

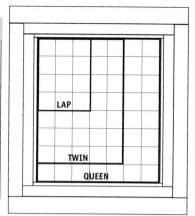

Fabric Requirements (42" wide, in yards)

	LAP	TWIN	QUEEN
Fabric #1, Background—Pieces A, B, C	1 1/4	2 3/4	4 1/4
Fabric #2, 1st Medium—Pieces D & E	7/8	1 7/8	2 3/4
Fabric #3, 2nd Medium—Pieces F & G	3/4	1 3/8	2 1/4
Fabric #4, Focus—Piece H	5/8	1 1/8	1 5/8
Inner Border	1/3	1/2	5/8
Middle Border	1/2	5/8	3/4
Outer Border	7/8	1 1/4	1 1/2
Binding	3/8	5/8	3/4
Backing Fabric	3 1/8	5 7/8	7 1/4

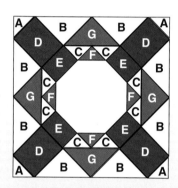

**All Kinds Block
#3072**

All Kinds

Once in a Blue Moon, 50" x 62"
12" blocks (12), three borders

Joan Schopp Hunn, Duluth, MN
quilted by Carolyn Napper, Beaver Bay, MN

Joan is a relatively new quilter with a great sense of color. She is a master gardener and was an urban planner, switching from planning cities to planning quilts. Joan is a precision piecer who has started to teach new quilters her techniques and tricks. She is also a new member of the Ladies of the Evening quilt group.

40

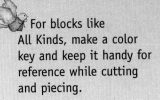

Cutting Instructions

Fabric #1, Background—Piece A			
Cut strips 2 5/8" x width of fabric	2	5	8
☐ Crosscut into 2 5/8" squares	24	70	112
◿ Crosscut diagonally once into half-square triangles	48	140	224

Fabric #1, Background—Piece B			
Cut strips 5 1/2" x width of fabric	4	10	16
☐ Crosscut into 5 1/2" squares	24	70	112
⊠ Crosscut diagonally twice into quarter-square triangles	96	280	448

Fabric #1, Background—Piece C			
Cut strips 3 3/8" x width of fabric	2	6	10
☐ Crosscut into 3 3/8" squares	24	70	112
⊠ Crosscut diagonally twice into quarter-square triangles	96	280	448

Fabric #2, 1st Medium—Piece D			
Cut strips 3" x width of fabric	4	12	19
☐ Crosscut into 3" x 3 1/2" rectangles	48	140	224

Fabric #2, 1st Medium—Piece E			
Cut strips 3" x width of fabric	3	7	11
☐ Crosscut into 3" x 2" rectangles	48	140	224

Fabric #3, 2nd Medium—Piece F			
Cut strips 2" x width of fabric	3	7	11
☐ Crosscut into 2" squares	48	140	224

Fabric #3, 2nd Medium—Piece G			
Cut strips 5 1/2" x width of fabric	2	5	8
☐ Crosscut into 5 1/2" squares	12	35	56
⊠ Crosscut diagonally twice into quarter-square triangles	48	140	224

Fabric #4, Focus—Piece H			
Cut strips 6" x width of fabric	2	5	8
☐ Crosscut into 6" squares	12	35	56

Inner Border			
Cut strips 1 1/2" x width of fabric	5	8	10

Middle Border			
Cut strips 2 1/2" x width of fabric	5	8	10

Outer Border			
Cut strips 4 1/2" x width of fabric	6	9	10

Binding			
Cut strips 2 1/4" x width of fabric	6	9	11

For blocks like All Kinds, make a color key and keep it handy for reference while cutting and piecing.

Piecing Directions

Read all the instructions before you begin.

Always place right sides of fabric together for stitching.

Use scant 1/4" seam allowances.

Press seam allowances in the direction of arrows.

1 Draw a pencil line corner to corner on the wrong side of all **Piece F**s.

Tip for Step 3

STITCH
RIGHT SIDE PIECE E
WRONG SIDE PIECE C

2 Place **Piece F** on corners of **Piece H**. Sew on the pencil line. Trim seam allowance to 1/4" as shown. Make **12(35,56)**. Press away from **Piece H**.

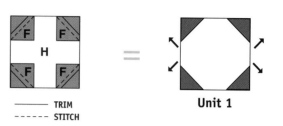

——— TRIM
- - - - STITCH

Unit 1

3 Sew **Piece C** to both sides of **Piece E** as shown. Make **48(140,224)**. Press. Trim.

C + E + C = Unit 2

4 Sew **Unit 2** to opposite sides of **Unit 1** as shown. Make **12(35,56)**. Press. Trim.

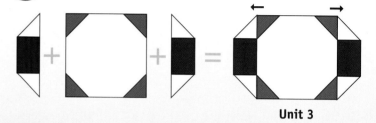

Unit 3

5 Sew remaining **Unit 2**s to opposite sides of **Unit 3** as shown. Make **12(35,56)**. Press. Trim.

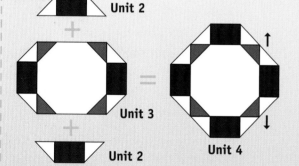

Unit 2
Unit 3
Unit 2
Unit 4

6 Sew **Piece G** to opposite sides of **Unit 4** as shown. Make **12(35,56)**. Press. Trim.

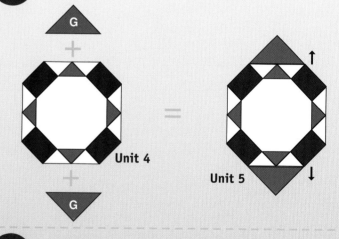

G
Unit 4
G
Unit 5

7 Sew remaining **Piece G**s to opposite sides of Unit 5 as shown. Make **12(35,56)**. Press.

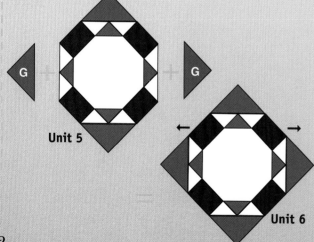

G
Unit 5
G
Unit 6

8 Sew **Piece B** to opposite sides of **Piece D**. Make **48(140,224)**. Press. Trim.

B + D + B = Unit 7

9 Sew **Piece A** to Unit 7 as shown. Make **48(140,224)**. Press. Trim.

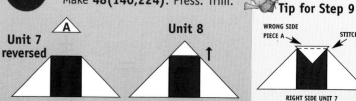

Unit 7 reversed
A
Unit 8

Tip for Step 9

WRONG SIDE PIECE A
STITCH
RIGHT SIDE UNIT 7

10 Sew **Unit 8** to opposite sides of **Unit 6** as shown. Make **12(35,56)**. Press. Trim.

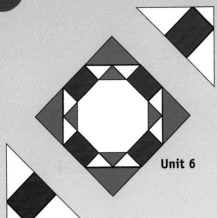

Unit 8

Unit 6

Unit 8

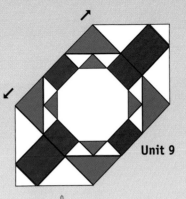

Unit 9

11 Sew remaining **Unit 8**s to opposite sides of **Unit 9** as shown. Make **12(35,56)**. Press.

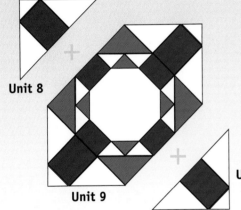

Unit 8

Unit 9

Unit 8

Tips for Steps 10 and 11

When you stitch **Unit 8** to **Unit 6** and **Unit 9**, butt, pin, and stitch exactly through the intersecting seams.

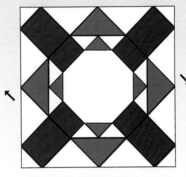

All Kinds Block

For precise points, always stitch directly through the intersecting seams of a triangle point, even if the seam allowance will not be exactly 1/4".

Quilt Assembly

◆ Lay out the blocks **3(5,7)** across and **4(7,8)** down. Rotate the blocks so pressed seams alternate directions and butt together.

◆ Before sewing, butt and pin intersecting seams.

◆ Follow the instructions on pages 134 and 135 for sewing blocks and rows together.

◆ Follow the directions on page 136 for adding borders.

Finishing the Quilt

◆ Follow the instructions on page 137 for making the quilt sandwich.

◆ Follow the instructions on page 137 for basting the quilt.

◆ Refer to page 137 for information on quilting.

◆ Follow the instructions on page 138 for binding the quilt.

All Kinds

It Takes All Kinds, 50" x 62"
12" blocks (12), three borders

Ardis Leland, Duluth, MN
hand quilted by Ardis Leland, Duluth, MN

Ardis has been quilting for about twenty years and is an excellent piecer. She makes many quilts each year and gives most of them away. She is extremely fond of hand quilting and uses this skill on most of her quilts.

Around the Corner

Sunrise, Sunset, 50" x 62"
12" blocks (12), 3 borders

Eileen Sugars, Duluth, MN
quilted by Jan Peterson, Solon Springs, WI

Artist's Secrets

In the last picture in The Quiltmaker's Gift, *the King is being told about needy children just around the corner while the Quiltmaker sews a quilt that blends Trip Around the World and Next-Door Neighbor. Our next-door neighbors are both around the corner and around the world.*

Around the Corner

Brackman/BlockBase Number: 2043
Earliest publication date: approximately 1936
Alternate names: none

Around the Corner appeared in a syndicated column written by Loretta Leitner Rising for the *Chicago Tribune*. The pseudonym Nancy Cabot was used for the column. The column began in 1932 and continued through the decade. Hundreds of Cabot patterns were grouped into booklet form and sold via mail order during the 1930s. The Spinning Wheel syndicate and the Progressive Farmer also sold the same patterns. The Cabot patterns were reprinted in the 1960s and 70s by several small publishers.

The center of the pattern can be classified as a square in a square in a square—a simple concept. However the next units become more complicated and it is important that precision pinning and piecing methods be used to guarantee a block with sharp intersections. The quilt example Flight Around the Square was a joint effort by the staff of Fabrics Plus in Marshall, MN. They all mastered the block and in addition to making blocks for the quilt they each made an additional block showcasing how the block would look using different fabrics.

Quiltmaker's Design Challenges

◆ Consider using juvenile prints or novelty fabrics. Carol Jean used a bright children's print in the quilt she made for her granddaughter Isabel Rose.

◆ For a rich, sophisticated look use oriental fabrics.

◆ Create a pieced border of the Flying Geese units.

◆ Experiment by reversing the medium and dark fabric placements.

◆ Consider using sashing and cornerstones between the blocks.

◆ For a dramatic look consider black-and-white fabrics for the background and bright, bold fabrics for the other pieces.

◆ Try quilting in the ditch around each piece. In one of the sample blocks on page 47, each piece was outlined with machine stitching 1/4" in from the seams.

Critical care nurse Eileen Sugars works nights in a cardiac intensive care unit in a local hospital. Until the last few years she hand pieced and hand quilted all her quilts. Jan Peterson bought her long-arm quilting machine just over a year ago and has been busy perfecting her skills. Jan is the daughter of Toni Gotelaere, who made the Grandmother's Flower Garden for this book.

By day the quiltmaker sewed the beautiful quilts she would not sell, and at night the king took them down to the town.

Quilt Information (finished size measurements)

	LAP	TWIN	QUEEN
Quilt Size without Borders	36" x 48"	60" x 84"	84" x 96"
Quilt Size with Borders	50" x 62"	74" x 98"	98" x 110"
Finished Block Size	12"	12"	12"
Number of Blocks	12	35	56
Block Layout	3 x 4	5 x 7	7 x 8
Backing Layout			

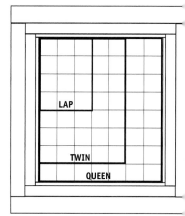

Fabric Requirements (42" wide, in yards)

	LAP	TWIN	QUEEN
Fabric #1, Light—Pieces A & B	3/4	1 1/2	2 1/4
Fabric #2, Dark—Piece C	5/8	1 1/8	1 5/8
Fabric #3, Focus—Pieces D & E	1 1/8	2 5/8	4 1/8
Fabric #4, Medium—Piece F	3/4	1 3/4	2 3/4
Inner Border	1/3	1/2	5/8
Middle Border	1/2	5/8	3/4
Outer Border	7/8	1 1/4	1 1/2
Binding	3/8	5/8	3/4
Backing Fabric	3 1/8	5 7/8	7 1/4

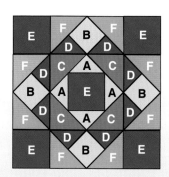

**Around the Corner Block
#2043**

Around the Corner

Who's Around the Corner—Lions, Tigers & Pigs? O My!
50" x 62", 12" blocks (12), 3 mitered borders

Carol Jean Brooks, Duluth, MN
quilted by Sue Munns, Duluth, MN

*Carol Jean is a retired surgical technician
who took up quilting when several coworkers
brought their quilt blocks to hand piece during
breaks. Carol Jean makes only comfort quilts
that she gives away to whomever needs some
intensive TLC. She made this quilt for her latest
grandchild, Isabel Rose. Sue Munns has had a
long-arm quilting machine for many years.
Since her work was published in the last book,
she gets requests for her services from as far
away as Alaska.*

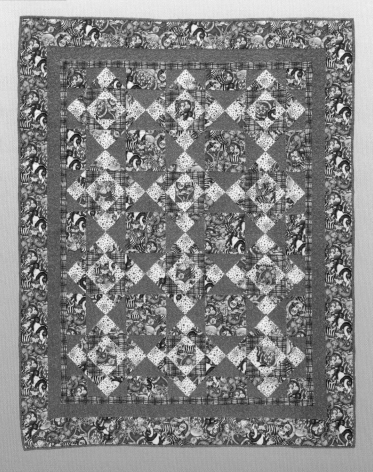

Cutting Instructions

	LAP	TWIN	QUEEN
Fabric #1, Light—Piece A			
Cut strips 4 1/4" x width of fabric	2	4	7
☐ Crosscut into 4 1/4" squares	12	35	56
☒ Crosscut diagonally twice into quarter-square triangles	48	140	224
Fabric #1, Light—Piece B			
Cut strips 2 5/8" x width of fabric	4	10	15
☐ Crosscut into 2 5/8" squares	48	140	224
Fabric #2, Dark—Piece C			
Cut strips 3 7/8" x width of fabric	3	7	12
☐ Crosscut into 3 7/8" squares	24	70	112
◪ Crosscut diagonally once into half-square triangles	48	140	224
Fabric #3, Focus—Piece D			
Cut strips 4 1/4" x width of fabric	3	8	13
☐ Crosscut into 4 1/4" squares	24	70	112
☒ Crosscut diagonally twice into quarter-square triangles	96	280	448
Fabric #3, Focus—Piece E			
Cut strips 3 1/2" x width of fabric	5	15	24
☐ Crosscut into 3 1/2" squares	60	175	280
Fabric #4, Medium—Piece F			
Cut strips 3 7/8" x width of fabric	5	14	23
☐ Crosscut into 3 7/8" squares	48	140	224
◪ Crosscut diagonally once into half-square triangles	96	280	448
Inner Border			
Cut strips 1 1/2" x width of fabric	5	8	10
Middle Border			
Cut strips 2 1/2" x width of fabric	5	8	10
Outer Border			
Cut strips 4 1/2" x width of fabric	6	9	10
Binding			
Cut strips 2 1/4" x width of fabric	6	9	11

For blocks like Around the Corner, make a color key and keep it handy for reference while cutting and piecing.

For precise points, always stitch directly through the intersecting seams of a triangle point, even if the seam allowance will not be exactly 1/4".

These squares show how the choice of fabric can give a block an entirely different look. They were made by Carol Hinz, Carol Clark, Lucy Hefti, and Patricia Seeklander of Marshall, MN.

Joanne's Around the Corner class sampler.

Piecing Directions

1 Sew **Piece A** to opposite sides of **Piece E** as shown. Make **12(35,56)**. Press. Trim dog-ears.

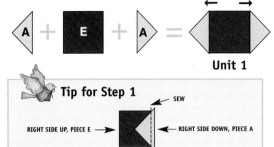

Unit 1

Tip for Step 1

RIGHT SIDE UP, PIECE E → ← RIGHT SIDE DOWN, PIECE A — SEW

2 Sew remaining **Piece A**s to opposite sides of **Unit 1** as shown. Make **12(35,56)**. Press. Trim dog-ears.

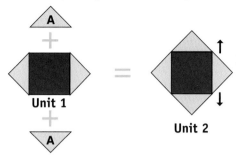

Unit 1

Unit 2

3 Sew **Piece C** to opposite sides of **Unit 2** as shown. Make **12(35,56)**. Press. Trim dog-ears.

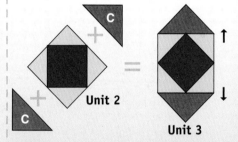

Unit 2

Unit 3

4 Sew remaining **Piece C**s to opposite sides of **Unit 3** as shown. Make **12(35,56)**. Press. Trim dog-ears.

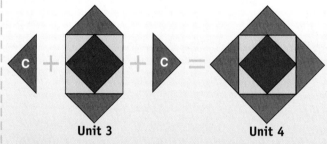

Unit 3 + **Unit 3** + = **Unit 4**

Tip for Step 5

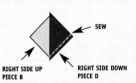

SEW

RIGHT SIDE UP PIECE B — RIGHT SIDE DOWN PIECE D

Tip for Step 6

RIGHT SIDE DOWN PIECE D

RIGHT SIDE UP UNIT 5

SEW

5 Sew **Piece D** to **Piece B** as shown. Make **48(140,224)**. Press.

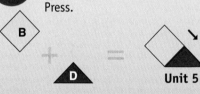

B + D = **Unit 5**

6 Sew remaining **Piece D**s to **Unit 5** as shown. Make **48(140,224)**. Press. Trim dog-ears.

D + = **Unit 6**

Tip for Step 7

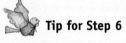

RIGHT SIDE DOWN PIECE F

RIGHT SIDE UP UNIT 6

SEW

7 Sew **Piece F** to **Unit 6** as shown. Make **48(140,224)**. Press.

8 Sew remaining **Piece F**s to **Unit 7** as shown. Make **48(140,224)**. Press. Trim dog-ears.

    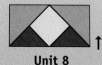

F + **Unit 6** = **Unit 7**   **Unit 7** + F = **Unit 8**

Tip for Step 8

SEW

RIGHT SIDE UP UNIT 7

RIGHT SIDE DOWN PIECE F

9 Sew **Unit 8** to opposite sides of **Unit 4** as shown. Make **12(35,56)**. Press.

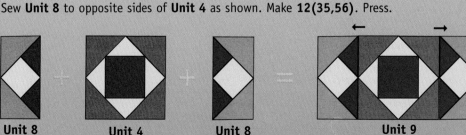

Unit 8   **Unit 4**   **Unit 8**   **Unit 9**

10

Sew remaining **Piece E**s to opposite sides of **Unit 8** as shown. Make **24(70,112)**. Press.

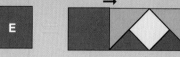

Unit 8

Unit 10

11

Sew **Unit 10** to opposite sides of **Unit 9**. Make **12(35,56)**. Press.

Unit 10

Unit 9

Unit 10 turned

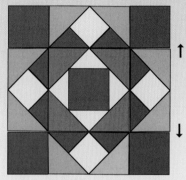

Around the Corner Block

Quilt Assembly

◆ Lay out the blocks **3(5,7)** across and **4(7,8)** down. Rotate the blocks so pressed seams alternate directions and butt together.

◆ Before sewing, butt and pin intersecting seams.

◆ Follow the instructions on pages 134 and 135 for sewing the blocks and rows together.

◆ Follow the instructions on page 136 for adding borders.

Finishing the Quilt

◆ Follow the instructions on page 137 for making the quilt sandwich.

◆ Follow the instructions on page 137 for basting the quilt.

◆ Refer to page 137 for information on quilting.

◆ Follow the instructions on page 138 for binding the quilt.

Around the Corner

Flight Around the Square, 50" x 62"
12" blocks (12), with sashing, cornerstones, and three borders

Elaine Nyquist, Carol A. Clark, Lucy Hefti, Carol J. Hinz, and Patricia Seeklander
quilted by Cindy Larson

Elaine, who owns Fabrics Plus in Marshall, MN, asked if she and her staff could make a quilt for this book. I was thrilled to have such an enthusiastic group of women participate. They not only made the bright and cheerful Flight Around the Square, they also made individual blocks. Pat and Lucy hand quilted their blocks, and the two Carols did machine quilting. The word must be out that I'm partial to pansies because several quiltmakers chose to do their quilts in a variety of pansy fabrics.

49

Hither & Yon

Flowers for the Soul, 62" x 86"
12" blocks (24), 3 plain borders

Joanne Larsen Line, Duluth, MN
quilted by Karen McTavish, Duluth, MN

Hither & Yon

Brackman/BlockBase Number: 2131

Earliest published example: *Farm Journal*

Alternate names: Spool

The *Farm Journal* was a periodical established in March of 1877. They absorbed at least three other pattern sources including *Country Gentlemen*, *The Farmer's Wife* and *Household Journal*. In the twentieth century they offered mail-order patterns and booklets. Some of the patterns are reproduced in Rachel Martin's *Modern Patchwork*, published by Countryside Press of Philadelphia in 1970.

Hither and Yon is a pattern for intermediate quilters and requires paying close attention to the piecing directions. There are several possible quilt layouts for this pattern. One of the examples is made entirely of scraps and also features a fun border. Another features pansy fabric, and the featured quilt also uses floral fabrics.

Artist's Secrets

The Quiltmaker had to search a while to find the king. That was not because the sparrow had neglected to tell her where the king was, but because Jeff had put hummingbirds into the story. Since hummingbirds don't live in Europe, I had them begin to follow her as she searched for the king. So since she looked for him in America, she might as well look in Australia and find him in China.

Quiltmaker's Design Challenge

◆ Try making an overall scrappy quilt paying close attention to value rather than color.

◆ Make half the blocks with light and dark backgrounds as shown in Here Kitty, Kitty.

◆ Experiment using two different darks for Pieces E and F.

◆ Incorporate one of the block elements for an exciting border treatment.

◆ Use a design wall and try reversing the block placements to create different looks.

◆ Try using a funky fabric for Piece D, such as an animal print or red-hot chili peppers.

. . . the king slowly emptied his wagons, trading his treasures for smiles around the world.

Joanne is trying to break away from her usual purples and instead chose peach and blues for this quilt. Karen did trapunto, crosshatching, and straight quilting to enhance this beautiful quilt.

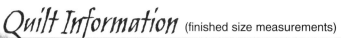

Quilt Information (finished size measurements)

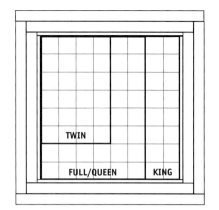

	TWIN	FULL/QUEEN	KING
Quilt Size without Borders	48" x 72"	72" x 96"	96" x 96"
Quilt Size with Borders	62" x 86"	86" x 110"	110" x 110"
Finished Block Size	12"	12"	12"
Number of Blocks	24	48	64
Block Layout	4 x 6	6 x 8	8 x 8
Backing Layout			

Fabric Requirements (42" wide, in yards)

	TWIN	FULL/QUEEN	KING
Fabric #1, Light—Piece A & B	2 5/8	4 3/4	6 3/8
Fabric #2, Accent—Piece C	5/8	3/4	1
Fabric #3, Focus—Piece D	2/3	7/8	1 3/8
Fabric #4, Dark—Piece E	1	1 1/2	2
Fabric #5, Medium—Piece F	1	1 7/8	2 1/2
Inner Border	1/3	1/2	5/8
Middle Border	1/2	5/8	7/8
Outer Border	7/8	1 1/3	1 5/8
Binding	5/8	7/8	1
Backing Fabric	3 1/3	6 1/8	7 7/8

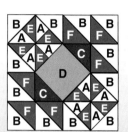

**Hither & Yon Block
#2131**

Hither & Yon

Passion for Pansies, 86" x 110"
12" blocks (48), 3 plain borders

Stephanie Orlowski, Cloquet, MN
quilted by Pam Stolan, Duluth, MN

Stephanie is a precision piecer—a requirement for making this quilt. She also shares Joanne's love of purples and pansies. Note the beautiful label she made for her quilt. Stephanie still works as a warehouse supervisor in an industrial safety business, but since the last book, she has added quilt teaching to her already busy schedule. Pam does the machine quilting on all Stephanie's quilts. They work together to pick out the quilting designs that will best enhance the pattern.

Cutting Instructions

	TWIN	FULL/QUEEN	KING
Fabric #1, Light—Piece A			
Cut strips 4 1/4" x width of fabric	6	11	15
☐ Crosscut into 4 1/4" squares	48	96	128
☒ Crosscut diagonally twice into quarter-square triangles	192	384	512
Fabric #1, Light—Piece B			
Cut strips 3 7/8" x width of fabric	15	29	39
☐ Crosscut into 3 7/8" squares	144	288	384
◪ Crosscut diagonally once into half-square triangles	288	576	768
Fabric #2, Accent—Piece C			
Cut strips 3 7/8" x width of fabric	3	5	7
☐ Crosscut into 3 7/8" squares	24	48	64
◪ Crosscut diagonally once into half-square triangles	48	96	128
Fabric #3, Focus—Piece D			
Cut strips 4 3/4" x width of fabric	3	6	8
☐ Crosscut into 4 3/4" squares	24	48	64
Fabric #4, Dark—Piece E			
Cut strips 4 1/4" x width of fabric	6	11	15
☐ Crosscut into 4 1/4" squares	48	96	128
☒ Crosscut diagonally twice into quarter-square triangles	192	384	512
Fabric #5, Medium—Piece F			
Cut strips 3 7/8" x width of fabric	8	15	20
☐ Crosscut into 3 7/8" squares	72	144	192
◪ Crosscut diagonally once into half-square triangles	144	288	384
Inner Border			
Cut strips 1 1/2" x width of fabric	6	9	10
Middle Border			
Cut strips 2 1/2" x width of fabric	6	8	10
Outer Border			
Cut strips 4 1/2" x width of fabric	7	9	10
Binding			
Cut strips 2 1/4" x width of fabric	7	10	11

For blocks like Hither & Yon, make a color key and keep it handy for reference while cutting and piecing.

Try using triangle paper to make **Unit 7**. You will still need to cut **7(14,19)** strips of **Piece B** to make **Units 5** and **6**.

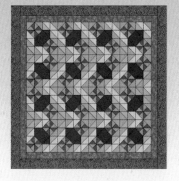

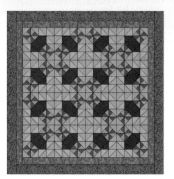

Dee Wojciehowski of Cloquet, MN, tests Hither & Yon at right. Three of her computer-aided layout designs for the pattern appear at far right. Dee uses BlockBase and Electric Quilt 5.

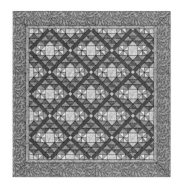

Piecing Directions

The Quiltmaker says . . .

Read all the instructions before you begin.

Always place right sides of fabric together for stitching.

Use scant 1/4" seam allowances.

Press seam allowances in the direction of arrows.

1 Sew **Piece C** to opposite sides of **Piece D** as shown. Make **24(48,64)**. Press. Trim dog-ears.

Unit 1

2 Sew **Piece A** to **Piece E** as shown. Make **96(192,256)**. Press. Trim dog-ears.

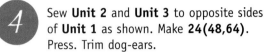

Unit 2

3 Sew **Piece E** to **Piece A** as shown. Make **96(192,256)**. Press. Trim dog-ears.

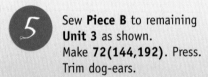

Unit 3

4 Sew **Unit 2** and **Unit 3** to opposite sides of **Unit 1** as shown. Make **24(48,64)**. Press. Trim dog-ears.

Unit 3

Unit 2 turned

Unit 4

5 Sew **Piece B** to remaining **Unit 3** as shown. Make **72(144,192)**. Press. Trim dog-ears.

Unit 3   **Unit 5**

6 Sew **Piece B** to remaining **Unit 2** as shown. Make **72(144,192)**. Press. Trim dog-ears.

Unit 2   **Unit 6**

7 Sew **Piece F** to **Piece B** as shown. Make **144(288,384)**. Press. Trim dog-ears.

Unit 7

8 Sew **Unit 5**, **Unit 5 (turned)**, **Unit 7** and **Unit 7** together as shown to make **Row 1**. Make **24(48,64)**. Press.

Unit 5   **Unit 5 turned**   **Unit 7**   **Unit 7**   **Row 1**

9 Sew **Unit 5** to **Unit 7** as shown. Make **24(48,64)**. Press.

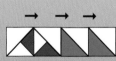

Unit 5

Unit 7

Unit 8

10 Sew **Unit 6** to **Unit 7** as shown. Make **24(48,64)**. Press.

Unit 7

Unit 6

Unit 9

11 Sew **Unit 8**, **Unit 4** and **Unit 9** as shown to make **Row 2**. Make **24(48,64)**. Press.

   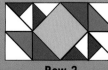

Unit 8   **Unit 4**   **Unit 9**   **Row 2**

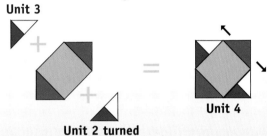

12 Sew **Unit 7**, **Unit 7**, **Unit 6** and **Unit 6 (turned)** together as shown to make **Row 3**. Make **24(48,64)**. Press.

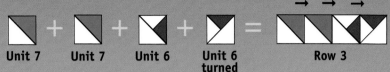

Unit 7   Unit 7   Unit 6   Unit 6 turned   Row 3

13 Sew **Rows 1**, **2** and **3** together as shown. Make **24(48,64)**. Press.

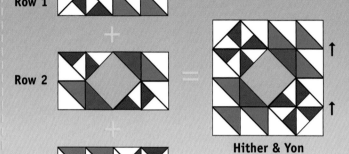

Row 1

Row 2

Row 3

Hither & Yon Block

For precise points, always stitch directly through the intersecting seams of a triangle point, even if the seam allowance will not be exactly 1/4".

Quilt Assembly

◆ Lay out the blocks **4(6,8)** across and **6(8,8)** down. These blocks are asymmetrical so be careful how you lay them out. Use a design wall and test the layout you prefer.

◆ Follow the instructions on pages 134 and 135 for sewing the blocks and rows together.

◆ Follow the instructions on page 136 for adding borders.

Finishing the Quilt

◆ Follow the instructions on page 137 for making the quilt sandwich.

◆ Follow the instructions on page 137 for basting the quilt.

◆ Refer to page 137 for information on quilting.

◆ Follow the instructions on page 138 for binding the quilt.

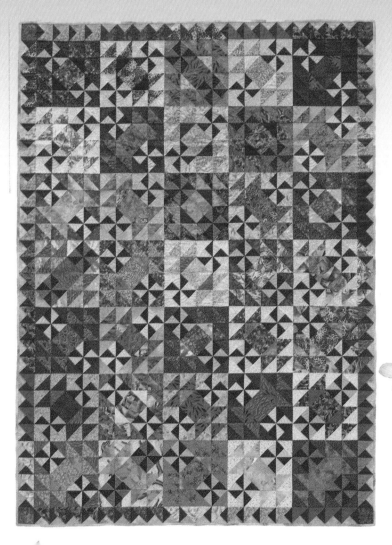

Hither & Yon

Here Kitty, Kitty, 64" x 80"
12" blocks (35), 1 pieced border

Maggie Brilla, Superior, WI
quilted by Angie Haworth, Superior, WI

Maggie is a woman of diverse skills and talents. She makes beautiful pieced and appliquéd quilts. Note the unique look she achieved using scraps for this pattern. However, there is another side to Maggie —her business card reads, "Have bull—will travel." Yes, Maggie owns an artificial insemination service. Angie, who has won numerous quilting awards, did the machine quilting.

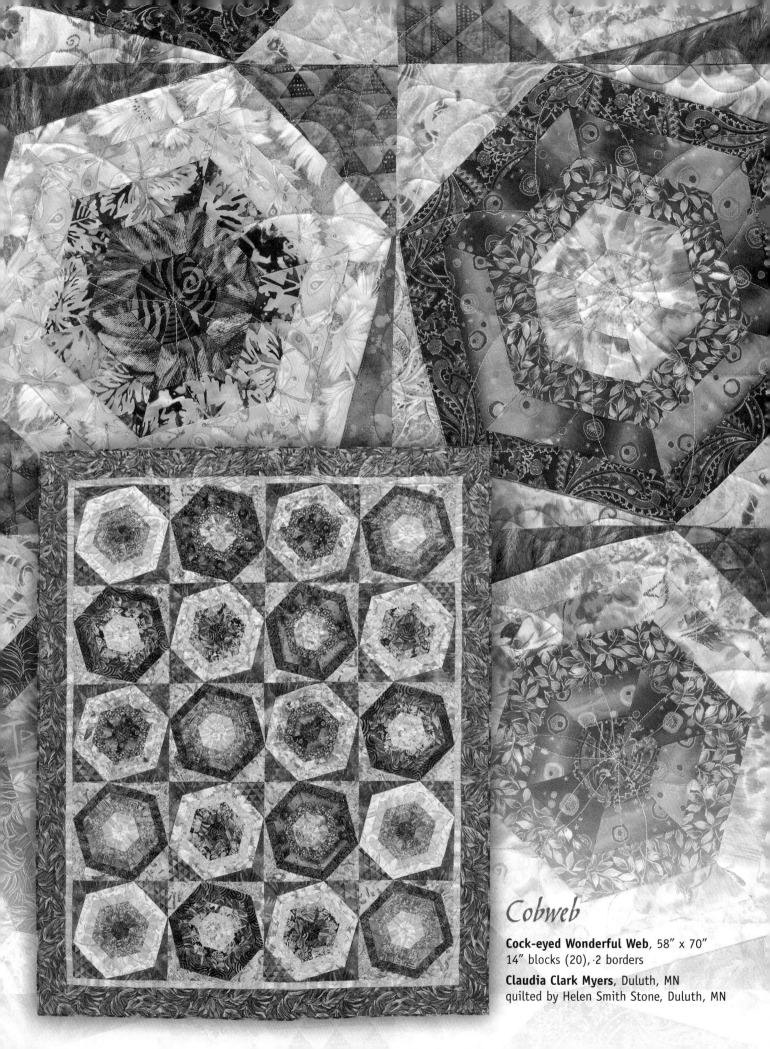

Cobweb

Cock-eyed Wonderful Web, 58" x 70"
14" blocks (20), 2 borders

Claudia Clark Myers, Duluth, MN
quilted by Helen Smith Stone, Duluth, MN

Cobweb

Cobweb

Brackman/BlockBase Number: 247

Earliest publication date: 1898 (Ladies' Art Company #353)

Alternate names: A Hexagon, Spider Web, An Old Fashion Wheel Quilt, and Hexagon Beauty

The Cobweb is a versatile block dating back to at least 1898. The block is divided into six equal segments. There are many interpretations of this block calling for the use of various numbers of fabrics. Claudia Clark Myers updated the pattern in this book incorporating secondary and tertiary patterns to create a block that makes an exciting quilt.

A new technique is introduced in this pattern. Sewing strata's and cutting wedges is a relatively simple task if the instructions provided are followed. The resulting quilt will be stunning.

Claudia, who was a costume designer for over twenty-five years, retired to make award-winning quilts. She designed this Cobweb based on Gail de Marcken's illustration in The Quiltmaker's Gift. *Helen, who was the first person in the Duluth area to start a long-arm quilting business, did the machine quilting.*

Artist's Secrets

The Cobweb pattern is featured when the king yields to the Quiltmaker's proposal. She designed the trap much earlier in the book, making a quilt with this pattern with the help of a golden spider. I think of this pattern as "Gotcha."

Quiltmaker's Design Challenges

◆ Try using Amish colors with several different black background fabrics.

◆ The background fabrics create a secondary and tertiary pattern over the entire quilt top. How could you use this quality to create more visual interest?

◆ Try reversing the wedges to look like Rita's quilt on page 63.

◆ Choose a border fabric to frame your quilt. Rita used a border fabric from *The Quiltmaker's Gift* fabric line to tie her quilt together.

◆ Make more than three different stratas for a truly scrappy look.

◆ Incorporate geometric fabric in the stratas to add more jazz to your quilt.

" . . . give away all of the things you own and I'll sew a quilt for you. And with each gift that you give, I'll add another piece to your quilt."

Quilt Information (finished size measurements)

	LAP	TWIN	QUEEN
Quilt Size without Borders	40 1/2" x 54"	54" x 67 1/2"	81" x 94 1/2"
Quilt Size with Borders	50 1/2" x 64"	64" x 77 1/2"	91" x 104 1/2"
Finished Block Size	13 1/2"	13 1/2"	13 1/2"
Number of Blocks	12	20	42
Block Layout	3 x 4	4 x 5	6 x 7
Backing Layout	←→ ←→	←→ ←→	←→ ←→ ←→ ←→

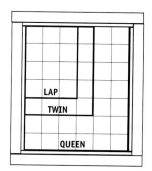

Fabric Requirements (42" wide, in yards)

	LAP	TWIN	QUEEN
Fabric #1, Light Background #1—Pieces A & Ar	3/8	1/2	7/8
Fabric #2, Light Background #2—Piece A & Ar	3/8	1/2	7/8
Fabric #3, Light Background #3—Piece B	1/3	5/8	3/4
Fabric #4, Medium Background #1—Pieces A & Ar	3/8	1/2	7/8
Fabric #5, Medium Background #2—Pieces A & Ar	3/8	1/2	7/8
Fabric #6, Medium Background #3—Piece B	1/3	5/8	3/4
Fabric #7, Light for Strata #1—Piece C	1/4	1/3	2/3
Fabric #8, Medium Light for Strata #1—Piece D	1/4	1/3	2/3
Fabric #9, Medium for Strata #1—Piece E	1/4	1/3	2/3
Fabric #10, Medium Dark for Strata #1—Piece F	1/4	1/3	2/3
Fabric #11, Dark for Strata #1—Piece G	1/4	1/3	2/3
Fabric #12, Light for Strata #2—Piece C	1/4	1/3	2/3
Fabric #13, Medium Light for Strata #2—Piece D	1/4	1/3	2/3
Fabric #14, Medium for Strata #2—Piece E	1/4	1/3	2/3
Fabric #15, Medium Dark for Strata #2—Piece F	1/4	1/3	2/3
Fabric #16, Dark for Strata #2—Piece G	1/4	1/3	2/3
Fabric #17, Light for Strata #3—Piece C	1/4	1/3	2/3
Fabric #18, Medium Light for Strata #3—Piece D	1/4	1/3	2/3
Fabric #19, Medium for Strata #3—Piece E	1/4	1/3	2/3
Fabric #20, Medium Dark for Strata #3—Piece F	1/4	1/3	2/3
Fabric #21, Dark for Strata #3—Piece G	1/4	1/3	2/3
Fabric #22, Inner Border	1/3	1/2	1/2
Fabric #23, Outer Border	1	1 1/8	1 3/8
Fabric #24, Binding	1/2	5/8	3/4
Backing Fabric	2 5/8	3 1/3	6 1/8

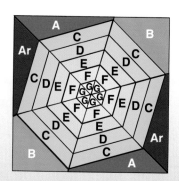

Cobweb Block #247

Nonquilters Deb Lutkevich and Carlene Sippola check out Joanne's Cobweb quilt and the label.

Cutting Instructions

	LP	TW	QN
Fabric #1, Light Background #1—Pieces A/Ar Cut strips 3-1/8" x width of fabric	2	4	7
Fabric #2, Light Background #2—Pieces A/Ar Cut strips 3-1/8" x width of fabric	2	4	7
Fabric #3, Light Background #3—Piece B Cut strips 5-7/8" x width of fabric	1	2	3
☐ Crosscut into 5-7/8" squares	6	10	21
☑ Crosscut diagonally into half-square triangles	12	20	42
Fabric #4, Medium Background #1—Pieces A/Ar Cut strips 3-1/8" x width of fabric	2	4	7
Fabric #5, Medium Background #2—Pieces A/Ar Cut strips 3-1/8" x width of fabric	2	4	7
Fabric #6, Medium Background #3—Piece B Cut strips 5-7/8" x width of fabric	1	2	3
☐ Crosscut into 5-7/8" squares	6	10	21
☑ Crosscut diagonally into half-square triangles	12	20	42
Fabric #7, Light for Strata #1—Piece C Cut strips 1-3/4" x width of fabric	3	5	10
Fabric #8, Medium Light for Strata #1—Piece D Cut strips 1-3/4" x width of fabric	3	5	10
Fabric #9, Medium for Strata #1—Piece E Cut strips 1-3/4" x width of fabric	3	5	10
Fabric #10, Medium Dark for Strata #1—Piece F Cut strips 1-3/4" x width of fabric	3	5	10
Fabric #11, Dark for Strata #1—Piece G Cut strips 1-3/4" x width of fabric	3	5	10
Fabric #12, Light for Strata #2—Piece C Cut strips 1-3/4" x width of fabric	3	5	10

	LP	TW	QN
Fabric #13, Medium Light for Strata #2—Piece D Cut strips 1-3/4" x width of fabric	3	5	10
Fabric #14, Medium for Strata #2—Piece E Cut strips 1-3/4" x width of fabric	3	5	10
Fabric #15, Medium Dark for Strata #2—Piece F Cut strips 1-3/4" x width of fabric	3	5	10
Fabric #16, Dark for Strata #2—Piece G Cut strips 1-3/4" x width of fabric	3	5	10
Fabric #17, Light for Strata #3—Piece C Cut strips 1-3/4" x width of fabric	3	5	10
Fabric #18, Medium Light for Strata #3—Piece D Cut strips 1-3/4" x width of fabric	3	5	10
Fabric #19, Medium for Strata #3—Piece E Cut strips 1-3/4" x width of fabric	3	5	10
Fabric #20, Medium Dark for Strata #3—Piece F Cut strips 1-3/4" x width of fabric	3	5	10
Fabric #21, Dark for Strata #3—Piece G Cut strips 1-3/4" x width of fabric	3	5	10
Fabric #22, Inner Border Cut strips 1-1/2" x width of fabric	5	7	9
Fabric #23, Outer Border Cut strips 4-1/2" x width of fabric	6	7	10
Fabric #24, Binding Fabric Cut strips 2-1/4" x width of fabric	6	7	10

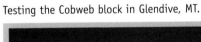

Testing the Cobweb block in Glendive, MT.

For blocks like Cobweb, make a color key and keep it handy for reference while cutting and piecing.

Piecing Directions

1 For **Strata #1** sew **Piece C, D, E, F** and **G** together as shown. For straight stratas, sew **Piece C** to **D** from left to right as shown below. Sew **Piece D** to **E** from right to left. Sew **Piece E** to **F** from left to right. Sew **Piece F** to **G** from right to left. Make **3(5,10)**. Press **1 1/2(2 1/2,5)** stratas toward **Piece G**. Press **1 1/2(2-1/2,5)** stratas toward **Piece C**.

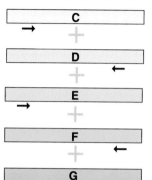

Strata 1   Strata 1

2 Use a **60° ruler** with 1/4" increments to cut the wedges. Place the **6 3/4"** line of the ruler directly on the bottom straight edge of **Strata #1**. The 60° angle of the ruler will be exactly on the top edge of the strata. Carefully cut strata along both sides as shown below. Piece cut will be a 60° wedge.

Strata 1   Wedge

3 Turn ruler and place the **6 3/4" line** directly on the top straight edge of **Strata #1** and have the **60° angle** exactly on the bottom edge as shown. Carefully cut another wedge. If necessary straighten the cut edge. Repeat this process to the end of the strata. Each strata will yield 9 cuts for a total of **27(45,90)** wedges. Separate the wedges into light and dark piles. There will be **12(20,40)** light wedges and **15(25,50)** dark wedges.

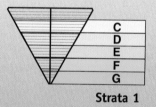

Strata 1    Wedge

4 Within the set of light wedges separate those pressed toward the outside edge and those pressed toward the point. Do the same for the dark wedges.

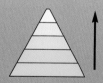

Dark Wedges

Light Wedges

5 Select **6 light wedges**, 3 pressed toward the outside edge and 3 pressed toward the point. Alternate the wedges as shown below. Pay close attention to the numbers assigned to the wedges. **Wedges 1, 3,** and **5** are pressed toward the outside. **Wedges 2, 4,** and **6** are pressed toward the center.

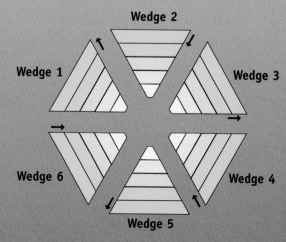

Wedge 2

Wedge 1   Wedge 3

Wedge 6   Wedge 4

Wedge 5

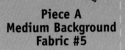

6 Using **Medium Background Fabric #4** and **Medium Background Fabric #5** place right sides together. Trace the **Cobweb template** on the wrong side as shown below. Trace and cut out **12(20,42)** sets. Each set yields **Piece A** and **Piece Ar**.

Medium Background Fabric #4, wrong side up

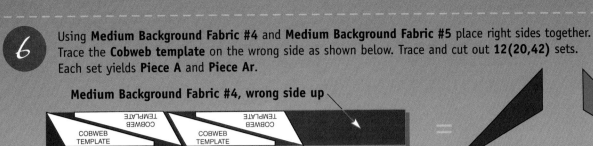

COBWEB TEMPLATE

COBWEB TEMPLATE

Medium Background Fabric #5, right side up

**Piece Ar
Medium Background
Fabric #4**

**Piece A
Medium Background
Fabric #5**

7 Using **Light Background Fabric #1** and **Light Background Fabric #2** place right sides together. Trace the **Cobweb template** on the wrong side as shown below. Trace and cut out **12(20,42)** sets. Each set yields **Piece A** and **Piece Ar**.

Light Background Fabric #1, wrong side up

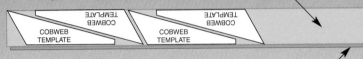

COBWEB TEMPLATE

COBWEB TEMPLATE

Light Background Fabric #2, right side up

**Piece Ar
Light Background
Fabric #1**

**Piece A
Light Background
Fabric #2**

8 Offset **Medium Background #4**, **Piece Ar** 1/4" as shown below and sew to **Wedges 1 and 4**. Press the seam in the same direction as the other seams in the wedge. Trim.

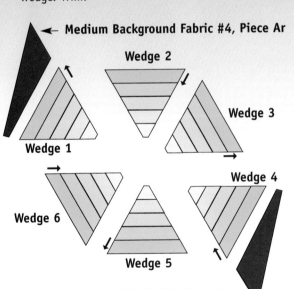

← **Medium Background Fabric #4, Piece Ar**

Wedge 2

Wedge 3

Wedge 1

Wedge 6

Wedge 4

Wedge 5

Medium Background Fabric #4, Piece Ar →

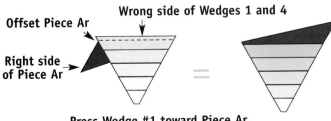

Wrong side of Wedges 1 and 4

Offset Piece Ar

**Right side
of Piece Ar**

**Press Wedge #1 toward Piece Ar.
Press Wedge #4 away from Piece Ar.**

9 Offset **Medium Background #5**, **Piece A** 1/4" as shown below and sew to **Wedges 2 and 5**. Press the seam in the same direction as the other seams in the wedge. Trim.

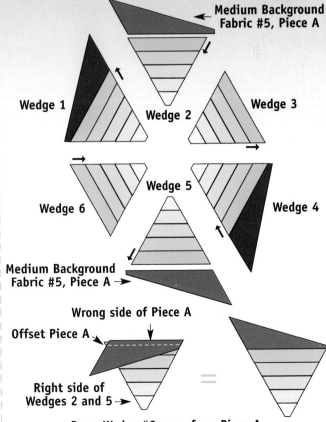

**Medium Background
Fabric #5, Piece A**

Wedge 1

Wedge 2

Wedge 3

Wedge 6

Wedge 5

Wedge 4

**Medium Background
Fabric #5, Piece A →**

Wrong side of Piece A

Offset Piece A

**Right side of
Wedges 2 and 5 →**

**Press Wedge #2 away from Piece A.
Press Wedge #5 toward Piece A.**

Piecing Directions continued

10 Sew **Medium Background Fabric #6, Piece B** to **Wedges 3 and 6** as shown. Press **Piece B** away from **Wedge 3** and towards **Wedge 6**. Trim.

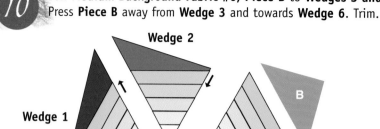

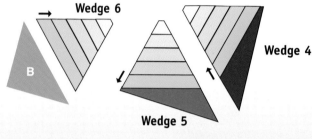

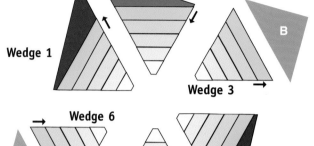

Wedges 3 and 6

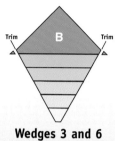

Wedges 3 and 6

11 Butt, pin, and sew the seams of **Wedge 1** and **Wedge 2** together. Press seam open.

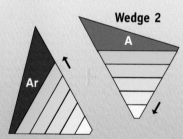

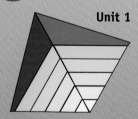

Unit 1

12 Butt, pin, and sew the seams of **Wedge 4** and **Wedge 5** together. Press seam open.

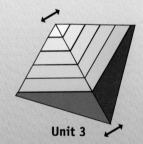

Unit 3

13 Butt, pin and sew **Wedge 3** to the right side of **Unit 1**. Press seam open.

Unit 1

+

Wedge 3

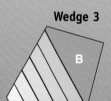

=

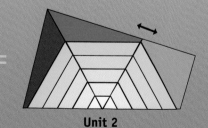

Unit 2

14 Sew **Wedge 6** to the left side of **Unit 3**. Press seams open.

Wedge 6

+

Unit 3

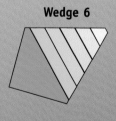

=

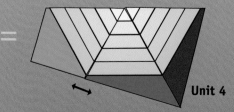

Unit 4

15 Align, pin and sew **Unit 2** to **Unit 4**. Press seam open.

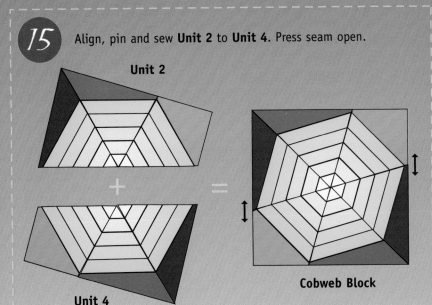

Unit 2

Unit 4

Cobweb Block

16 Repeat **Steps 5 through 15** to finish the remaining light wedges from **Strata 1**.

Repeat **Steps 5 through 15** to make the dark wedges from **Strata 1**. The dark wedges use **Light Background Fabric #2 Piece Ar** for **Wedges 1 and 4**, **Light Background Fabric #1 Piece A** for **Wedges 2 and 5** and **Light Background Piece Fabric #3** for **Piece B**.

Repeat **Step 1 through 4** to make **Stratas 2 and 3**.

Repeat **Steps 5 through 15** to complete the **Cobweb Blocks** using **Stratas 2 and 3**. Remember to use the **Medium Background** fabrics when making the light blocks and the **Light Background fabrics** when making the dark blocks.

Quilt Assembly

◆ Lay out the blocks **3(4,6)** across and **4(5,7)** down, alternating between the light and dark blocks.

◆ Follow the instructions on pages 134 and 135 for sewing the blocks and rows together. Press.

◆ Follow the instructions on page 136 for adding borders.

Finishing the Quilt

◆ Follow the instructions on page 137 for making the quilt sandwich.

◆ Follow the instructions on page 137 for basting the quilt.

◆ Refer to page 137 for information on quilting.

◆ Follow the instructions on page 138 for binding the quilt.

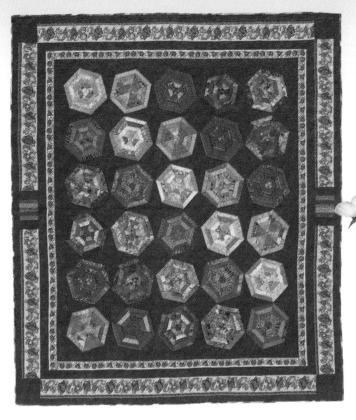

Cobweb

My Gifts, 78" x 90"
12" blocks (30), 4 borders

Rita Nau, Gibbon, MN
quilted by Rita Nau

Rita owns Gallagher's Quilt Shop and Café in Gibbon, MN, a store known for its contemporary fabrics and wonderful food and desserts. Rita used mostly fabric from the Quiltmaker's Gift line to make the cobwebs. She reversed the pieces so that each block has three stratas that run from dark to light and three that run from light to dark. This interpretation gives the blocks an interesting and totally different look.

63

Baby's Block

Baby's Got Blocks, 66" x 71"
5 1/4" x 6 1/2" blocks (120), one striped
and one plain border

Joanne Larsen Line, Duluth, MN
quilted by Angela Haworth, Superior, WI

Baby's Block

Brackman/BlockBase Number: 415.34

Earliest publication date: 1851 (*Godey's Lady's Book*)

Alternate names: Cube Work, Building Blocks, Cubes and Stars, Diamond Cube, Pandora's Box, Tumbling Blocks

The Baby's Block pattern has been around for many years. In 1851 it appeared as Godey Design in the *Godey's Lady's Book*. Carrie Hall and Rose G. Kretsinger, authors of *The Romance of the Patchwork Quilt in America*, featured the pattern in their book published in 1935 by Caxton Printers of Caldwell, ID. There have been numerous interpretations and names given to this block, but the basic elements are always the same. The Baby's Block belongs to the one-patch family of quilt blocks and creates the illusion of boxes.

A single block is made up of three 60° diamond shapes. A dramatic three-dimensional look is created by placing light, medium, and dark values in the same position in each block. The quilt Tumbling Together uses the same three fabrics throughout the entire quilt. Baby's Got Blocks uses several Kaffe Fassett stripes and a large number of Primrose Gradation fabrics as the lights and darks. The New Kid on the Block quilt uses many novelty fabrics and gives the impression of an I Spy quilt.

This pattern introduces the Y-seam and requires templates and attention to detail. It is essential that all pieces be marked and sewn together in the order stated. Pressing is also an important detail. However, once the block has been mastered it is very easy to make and can be quite addictive. I made at least 50 extra blocks, keeping going until I ran out of fabric. Thankfully common sense then prevailed.

Artist's Secrets

In my painting of a mother and her children, shown on page 67 of this book, the boy is my son Carl; the redhead is Natasha; and the baby is Paya. That makes the mother me, although my hair was never red.

Quiltmaker's Design Challenges

◆ Place the medium-value diamond at the top position.

◆ Place the dark-value diamond at the top position.

◆ Make a scrap Baby Block, keeping the lights, mediums, and darks in the same position.

◆ Feature a focus fabric in one of the diamonds. Or use reproduction fabrics to create an antique look.

◆ To quilt, try using a zigzag stitch around each diamond.

Joanne used Kaffe Fassett stripe fabrics for the medium color and a wide assortment of plain fabrics from Primrose Gradations for the lights and darks. Angie did the machine quilting on her commercial sewing machine. She outlined the medium and dark colors and did a freehand leaf pattern in the light area of the blocks. The straight line quilting in the outside border is unique and she filled in that area with freehand swirls.

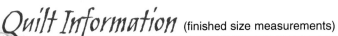

Quilt Information (finished size measurements)

	Wall Hanging	Lap	Queen
Quilt Size without Borders	26 1/4"x 33"	52 1/2"x 54"	84"x 87"
Quilt Size with Borders	36 1/4"x 43"	62 1/2"x 64"	94"x 97"
Finished Block Size	5 1/4"x 6"	5 1/4"x 6"	5 1/4"x 6"
Number of Blocks	35	120	304
Block Layout	5 x 7	10 x 12	16 x 19
Backing Layout			

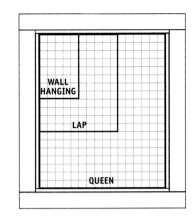

Fabric Requirements (42" wide, in yards)

	Wall Hanging	Lap	Queen
Fabric #1, Assorted Lights—Piece A & D	5/8	1 1/4	2 3/4
Fabric #2, Assorted Mediums—Piece B, G & E	3/4	1 3/8	2 3/4
Fabric #3, Assorted Darks—Pieces C, F, H & I	3/4	1 3/8	2 3/4
Inner Border	1/4	1/3	1/2
Outer Border	5/8	1	1 3/8
Binding	1/3	5/8	3/4
Backing Fabric	1 1/2	3 7/8	7 1/4

**Baby Block
#415.34**

Baby's Block

New Kid on the Block, 41" x 52"
5 1/4" x 6" blocks (50), 2 borders

Julie Owen, Superior, WI
quilted by Angela Haworth, Superior, WI

Julie made this quilt for a special young lady. Julie not only makes beautiful quilts, but she is also a master gardener. She is busy planning and designing gardens for her new home. Angie also designs and quilts clothing and has had two outfits in the Fairfield and Bernina Fashion Shows.

Cutting Instructions

	WALL HANGING	LAP	QUEEN
Fabric #1, Assorted Lights—Piece A			
Cut strips 3 1/8" x width of fabric	4	11	28
Crosscut using template on page 143	35	120	304
Fabric #1, Assorted Lights—Piece D			
Cut strips 2" x width of fabric	1	1	2
Crosscut using template on page 143	5	10	16
Fabric #2, Assorted Mediums—Piece B			
Cut strips 3 1/8" x width of fabric	4	11	28
Crosscut using template on page 143	35	120	304
Fabric #2, Assorted Mediums—Piece G			
Cut strip 3 1/8" x width of fabric	1	1	1
Crosscut using template on page 143	3	6	9
Fabric #2, Assorted Mediums—Piece I & E reversed			
Cut piece using template on page 143	1	1	1
Fabric #3, Assorted Darks—Piece C			
Cut strips 3 1/8" x width of fabric	4	11	28
Crosscut using template on page 143	35	120	304
Fabric #3, Assorted Darks—Piece F			
Cut strips 2" x width of fabric	1	1	2
Crosscut using template on page 143	5	10	16
Fabric #3, Assorted Darks—Piece H			
Cut strips 3 1/8" x width of fabric	1	1	1
Crosscut using template on page 143	3	6	9
Fabric #3, Assorted Darks—Piece I			
Cut piece using template on page 143	1	1	1
Inner Border			
Cut strips 1 1/2" x width of fabric	4	6	9
Outer Border			
Cut strips 4 1/2" x width of fabric	4	6	10
Binding			
Cut strips 2 1/4" x width of fabric	4	7	10

Baby's Block

Tumbling Together
5 1/4" x 6" blocks, two borders

Joe Provencher, Duluth, MN
quilted by Cindy Provencher, Duluth, MN

This is Joe's second quilt and he has plans to make many more. Joe is a postal worker by day, but in his spare time he enjoys the creativity and mathematical challenge of making three-dimensional quilts. He has all of his own quilting tools but still shares a sewing machine with his wife, Cindy. Cindy owns a long-arm quilting machine and works out of the fabric store Creations Unlimited in Duluth. This is their first joint venture. We'll keep our eyes open for more quilts from this talented husband and wife team.

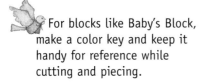
For blocks like Baby's Block, make a color key and keep it handy for reference while cutting and piecing.

Piecing Directions

The Quiltmaker says . . .

Read all the instructions before you begin.

Always place right sides of fabric together for stitching.

Use scant 1/4" seam allowances.

Press seam allowances in the direction of arrows.

It is necessary to use the pattern template provided to cut all the fabric pieces for this pattern. It is important to punch holes in the template at the intersections where the seam allowances cross. Place a pencil mark in every hole on the wrong side of every piece of fabric. There are several brands of commercial templates on the market and they should be available at your local quilt store. I used Set H from **Marti Michell's Perfect Patchwork Templates** to make Baby's Got Blocks.

1 With right sides together, align **Piece B (medium)** and **Piece A (light)** matching dots. Sew starting, stopping and backstitching 1/4" from each end at the dots. Make **35(120,304)**.

2 With right sides together, align **Piece C (dark)** with **Piece A (light)** matching dots. Sew starting, stopping and backstitching 1/4" from each end at the dots. Make **35(120,304)**.

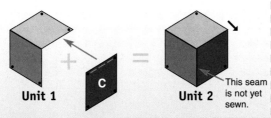

This seam is not yet sewn.

3 Fold **Piece A** of **Unit 2** in half with wrong sides together. Then, with right sides together, align **Piece C (dark)** with Piece **B (medium)** matching dots. Sew starting, stopping and backstitching 1/4" from each end at the dots. **Make 35(120,304)**.

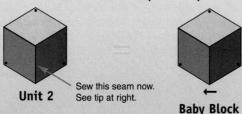

Unit 2

Sew this seam now. See tip at right.

Baby Block

4 Press all seam allowances in a circle by pressing **Piece B** toward **Piece A**, **Piece A** toward **Piece C** and **Piece C** toward **Piece B** as shown below.

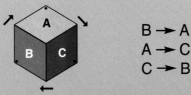

B → A
A → C
C → B

5 Use a design wall to lay out the blocks into rows. Add the setting pieces as shown in the diagrams.

Tips for Making Y-seams

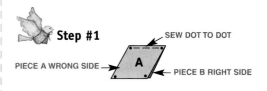
Step #1

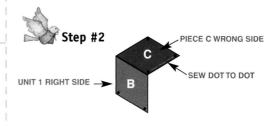
SEW DOT TO DOT
PIECE A WRONG SIDE
PIECE B RIGHT SIDE

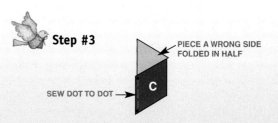
Step #2
PIECE C WRONG SIDE
SEW DOT TO DOT
UNIT 1 RIGHT SIDE

Step #3
PIECE A WRONG SIDE FOLDED IN HALF
SEW DOT TO DOT

 Always have the light diamond up.

 Start and stop sewing machine needle exactly at the dot.

 For a flat quilt, press seams in a circle around a central point.

 Use only mediums and darks for the corner pieces, **Piece I** and **Piece E**. Light pieces get lost in the overall design.

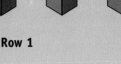

Quilt Assembly

Lay out the quilt in rows **5(10,16)** across and **7(12,19)** down. The light diamonds should always be on top.

1 Sew **Row 1** together starting, stopping and backstitching 1/4" from each end at the dots as shown. Sew **Piece G** to right side.

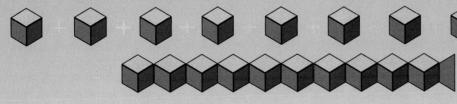

 G

Row 1

2 Sew **Piece I** to **Block 1** as shown. Sew **Piece F** to remaining blocks in **Row 1** as shown.

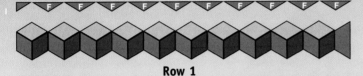

Row 1

Row 1

3 Starting with **Piece H**, sew **Row 2** together starting, stopping and backstitching 1/4" from each end at the dots as shown.

Row 2

4 Sew **Row 1** to **Row 2** together starting, stopping and backstitching 1/4" from each end at the dots as shown. Press in direction of arrows in diagram.

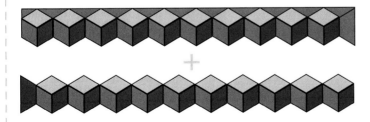

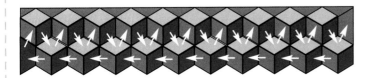

5 Continue to sew the individual rows together and to each other to complete the quilt top.

Wall Hanging

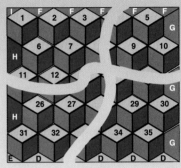

Lap

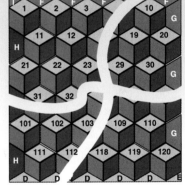

Queen

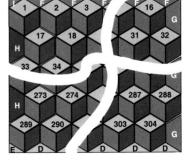

Follow the directions on page 136 for adding borders.

Finishing the Quilt

Follow the instructions on pages 137–138 for making and basting the quilt sandwich, hand or machine quilting, and binding.

Snowflake

Winter Wonderland, 50" x 62"
12" blocks (12), 3 borders

Joanne Larsen Line, Duluth, MN
quilted by Bonnie Jusczak,
Duluth, MN

Snowflake

Brackman/BlockBase Number: 2880
Earliest publication date: 1898 (Ladies' Art Company #277)
Alternate names: Cross Stitch, Snow Block, The Mountain Peak, Old Italian Design

This quilt is easy enough for children and beginners even though it does use a template to cut Piece C. The instructions for making the template are easy to follow and should not prove difficult for even the newest quilter. The pattern was originally made using a light, a dark, and an accent fabric. It introduces the quilter to cutting squares, quarter-square triangles, and making a template.

The pattern has a lot of possibilities depending on the fabrics chosen. The featured quilt gives the feeling of winter, and Austin's quilt gives the feeling of the tropics. Austin might know something about global warming.

Quiltmaker's Design Challenges

◆ Fussy cut Piece C from a special fabric or a border print.

◆ Consider using a stripe for Piece C.

◆ Chose a colorful focus fabric and use a variety of coordinating fabrics for Piece C.

◆ Try using reproduction fabrics to give the quilt an old-fashioned feel.

◆ Make a baby quilt with cute pastel flannels or vibrant juvenile primaries.

◆ Try a funky novelty with large images as your light fabric.

◆ Reverse the value placement of fabrics to create a light center radiating out to dark.

She would then take a newly finished quilt from her bag, wrap it around their shivering shoulders . . .

This fabric by Carol Enders for Benartex worked out beautifully for the Snowflake quilt. Bonnie incorporated faux trapunto quilting to highlight the snowflake pattern in the fabric. She also added candles to the design to provide warmth to a snowy day.

Artist's Secrets

Several things came into play when I chose this pattern. I was intrigued with how a pattern changes completely with your choice of fabric. The blues were batiks that form different "flakes" because of their patterns. I wanted a suggestion that the Quiltmaker had had a longtime friendship with the birds. I wanted to include a child. And I wanted another pattern that came from nature.

Snowflake

Leapin Lizzards, 50" x 62"
12" blocks (12), 2 borders, stripe sashing between blocks

Jessica and Austin Torvinen, Duluth, MN
quilted by Claudia Clark Myers, Duluth, MN

Award-winning quilter Jessica Torvinen mentored her son, Austin. Austin is ten years old and in the fifth grade at Lakewood Elementary School. Besides school, he enjoys playing basketball and soccer. He is on the snowboarding team at a local ski resort. He has a passion for jets and plans to be a pilot for the Air Force when he grows up. His grandmother Claudia Clark Myers did the machine quilting. She is not only an award-winning quilter, but she has designed a fabric line and a pattern line.

Quilt Information (finished size measurements)

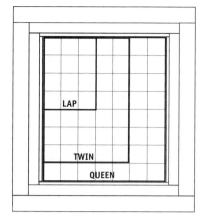

	LAP	TWIN	QUEEN
Quilt Size without Borders	36" x 48"	60" x 84"	84" x 96"
Quilt Size with Borders	50" x 62"	74" x 98"	98" x 110"
Finished Block Size	12"	12"	12"
Number of Blocks	12	35	56
Block Layout	3 x 4	5 x 7	7 x 8
Backing Layout			

Fabric Requirements (42" wide, in yards)

	LAP	TWIN	QUEEN
Fabric #1, Center—Piece A	1/2	1	1 1/4
Fabric #2, Background—Piece B	2/3	1 1/2	2 1/4
Fabric #3, Focus—Piece C*	1 1/2	3 3/8	5
Inner Border	1/3	1/2	5/8
Middle Border	1/2	3/4	7/8
Outer Border	1	1 3/8	1 1/2
Binding	1/2	2/3	7/8
Backing Fabric	3 1/8	5 7/8	7 1/4

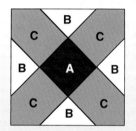

Snowflake Block #2880

*if you choose to use a border print you may need to purchase more fabric.

Cutting Instructions

Fabric #1, Center—Piece A			
Cut strips 4 3/4" x width of fabric	2	5	7
☐ Crosscut into 4 3/4" squares	12	35	56
Fabric #2, Background—Piece B			
Cut strips 7 1/4" x width of fabric	3	7	12
☐ Crosscut into 7 1/4" squares	12	35	56
☒ Crosscut diagonally twice into quarter-square triangles	48	140	224
Fabric #3, Focus—Piece C			
Cut strips 4 3/4" x width of fabric	8	24	38
☐ Crosscut into 4 3/4" x 7" rectangles	48	140	224
Use Snowflake template on page ** to finish the cut			
Inner Border			
Cut strips 1 1/2" x width of fabric	5	8	9
Middle Border			
Cut strips 2 1/2" x width of fabric	5	8	10
Outer Border			
Cut strips 4 1/2" x width of fabric	6	9	10
Binding			
Cut strips 2 1/4" x width of fabric	6	9	11

These blocks were made to test the Snowflake pattern at a workshop in Grand Rapids, MN—an amazing variety of "looks" from one pattern.

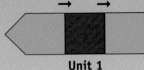

Piecing Directions

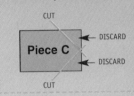 Finish cutting **Piece C** using **Snowflake template** on page 142. Make **48(140,224)**.

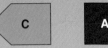

 Sew **Piece C** to opposite sides of **Piece A** as shown. Make **12(35,56)**. Press.

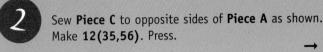

Unit 1

 Sew **Piece B** to opposite sides of remaining **Piece C**s. Make **24(70,112)**. Press. Trim.

Unit 2

For blocks like Snowflake, make a color key and keep it handy for reference while cutting and piecing.

Snowflake

Amethyst Crystals in the Snow, 50" x 62"
12" blocks (12), 1 border print

Joanne Larsen Line, Duluth, MN
quilted by Helen Smith Stone, Duluth, MN

A border print was fussy cut and used for Piece C creating a new design where the pieces joined. A soft blue floral print was used for the block center and a fossil fern was used for the background. Helen machine quilted an appropriate pattern to bring out highlights of the pattern design.

 Sew **Unit 2** to opposite sides of **Unit 1**. Make **12(35,56)**.

Unit 2

Unit 1

Unit 2 turned

Snowflake Block

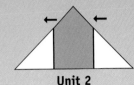

Quilt Assembly

◆ Lay out the blocks **3(5,7)** across and **4(7,8)** down. In each row rotate blocks so pressed seams butt nicely.

◆ Follow the directions on pages 134 and 135 for sewing the blocks and rows together.

◆ Follow the direction on page 136 for adding borders.

Finishing the Quilt

◆ Follow the instructions on page 137 for making the quilt sandwich.

◆ Follow the instructions on page 137 for basting the quilt.

◆ Refer to page 137 for information on quilting

◆ Follow the instructions on page 138 for binding the quilt.

Tree of Paradise

Winter Trees of Paradise, 62" x 87 1/2"
15" blocks (6 pieced, 2 plain),
one pieced border & one plain border

Judy Stingl Timm, Duluth, MN
quilted by Karen McTavish, Duluth, MN

Artist's Secrets

Tree of Paradise is such a lovely name.
As the king sat in the tree, he made a
decision that led to a paradise of happiness
for many people.

Tree of Paradise

Brackman/BlockBase Number: 819
Earliest Publication Date: 1895 (LAC #260)
Alternate names: Christmas Tree Patch, The Pine Tree,
Tree, Bay Tree

The Tree of Paradise block was first published by the
Ladies' Art Company and is listed in an 1895 catalog.
The Ladies' Art Company was founded in St. Louis by
H. M. Brockstedt and is credited as the first mail-order
quilt pattern company. There are many additional
patterns similar to the Tree of Paradise but what
differentiates them is the number of leaves. The Tree
of Life is perhaps the most popular pattern in this
grouping.

Triangle paper was used to make the leaves but
regular cutting instructions are provided for those who
do not wish to do so. The blocks are set on point
giving the quilt an updated look. Directions for the
border on the featured quilt have also been included.
The tree trunk and base have also been
simplified. In the featured quilt each block
uses a different combination of fabrics.
However, upon closer inspection you will
note the individual rows in each block are
the same fabric. The other quilt example uses
one single fabric but because of the varied
colors in the print the leaves appear to be
different.

Quiltmaker's Design Challenges

- Choose a color family such as green and make a planned
  scrappy version. Study a tree or look at a picture of a tree
  and note all the different values of green and where they
  occur on the tree.

- Straight set the blocks for a totally different look.

- Choose unique fabrics not always associated with trees,
  such as Judy did for her quilt.

- Appliqué or quilt a few birds into your tree. Joanne's quilt
  has a pair of birds quilted into the outside borders. The
  bird's tail feathers form giant fern fronds.

- Add additional width to the outer border to increase the
  overall size of quilt.

- Use a design wall to play with how the background fabric
  can provide a light source.

- Make a pieced border using half-square triangles or do a
  checkerboard pattern.

- Make a series of four wall hangings, one for each season
  of the year.

Judy Stingl Timm is a popular
teacher at Fabric Works in Superior, WI.
Judy loves picking out fabrics for quilts
and her color choices prove it. Her quilt
gives the effect of trees in the winter.
She loved the colors so much she
designed the border to continue the
look of an austere winter day in
northern Minnesota. Karen McTavish did
a multitude of quilting patterns to
enhance the beauty of the quilt.

. . . she was sitting on a tree limb sewing
tiny purple coats for all the sparrows.

75

Quilt Information (finished size measurements)

	WALL HANGING	TWIN	QUEEN
Quilt Size without Borders	42 1/2" x 42 1/2"	42 1/2" x 63 3/4"	63 3/4" x 85"
Quilt Size with Borders	62" x 62"	62" x 87 1/2"	87 1/2" x 113
Finished Block Size	15"	15"	15"
Number of Pieced Blocks	4	6	12
Number of Plain Blocks	1	2	6
Block Layout	2 x 2	2 x 3	3 x 4
Backing Layout			

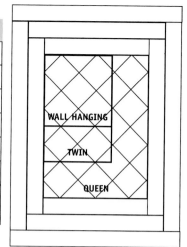

Fabric Requirements (42" wide, in yards)

	WALL HANGING	TWIN	QUEEN
Fabric #1, Assorted Light Backgrounds—Pieces A, B, C, & D/Dr	1 3/4	2 3/8	3 1/2
Fabric #2, Assorted Mediums & Darks—Pieces E, I & M	1 1/8	1 1/2	2 1/4
Fabric #3, Tree Branches—Piece F	3/8	3/8	3/8
Fabric #4, Tree Trunk—Pieces G & H	3/8	3/8	1/2
Fabric #5, Setting & Corner Triangles—Pieces J, K , & L	2	2 3/4	5 1/4
Top & Bottom Inner Border will use Fabric #5—yardage has been included above			
Pieced Border, will use Fabrics #1, 2 & 5—yardage has been included above			
Outer Border	1 1/4	1 1/3	1 7/8
Binding	1/2	1/2	5/8
Backing Fabric	3 7/8	5 1/4	6 1/2

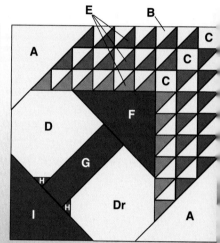

Tree of Paradise Block #819

Cutting Instructions

	WALL HANGING	TWIN	QUEEN
Fabric #1, Assorted Light Backgrounds—Piece A			
Cut strips 6 7/8" x width of fabric	3	4	5
☐ Crosscut into 6 7/8" squares	16	21	33
☑ Crosscut diagonally once into half-square triangles	32	42	66
Fabric #1, Assorted Light Backgrounds—Piece B			
Cut strips 2 3/8" x width of fabric	7	10	18
☐ Crosscut into 2 3/8" squares	110	155	275
☑ Crosscut diagonally once into half-square triangles	220	310	550
Fabric #1, Assorted Light Backgrounds—Piece C			
Cut strips 2" x width of fabric	1	1	2
☐ Crosscut into 2" squares	12	18	36
Fabric #1, Assorted Light Backgrounds—Piece D/Dr			
Cut strips 6 1/2" x width of fabric	2	2	4
With right sides of fabric together, trace template D/Dr on page 142 to the wrong side of the fabric.			
Cut sets using ruler as a guide. Yields sets of Piece D/Dr	4	6	12

Cutting Instructions *continued*

	WALL HANGING	TWIN	QUEEN
Fabric #2, Assorted Mediums & Darks—Piece E			
Cut strips 2 3/8" x width of fabric	9	13	22
☐ Crosscut into 2 3/8" squares	142	199	349
◺ Crosscut diagonally once into half-square triangles	284	398	698
Fabric #2, Tree Base—Piece I			
Cut strips 6 7/8" x width of fabric	1	1	1
☐ Crosscut into 6 7/8" squares	2	3	6
◺ Crosscut diagonally once into half-square triangles	4	6	12
Fabric #2, Assorted Mediums & Darks—Piece M			
Cut strips 3 7/8" x width of fabric	1	2	2
☐ Crosscut into 3 7/8" squares	10	13	19
◺ Crosscut diagonally once into half-square triangles	20	26	38
Fabric #3, Tree Branches—Piece F			
Cut strips 6 7/8" x width of fabric	1	1	1
☐ Crosscut into 6 7/8" squares	2	3	6
◺ Crosscut diagonally once into half-square triangles	4	6	12
Fabric #4, Tree Trunk—Piece G			
Cut strips 2 5/8" x width of fabric	1	1	2
☐ Crosscut into 2 5/8" x 6 7/8" rectangles	4	6	12
Fabric #4, Tree Trunk—Piece H			
Cut strips 1 7/8" x width of fabric	1	1	2
☐ Crosscut into 1 7/8" squares	8	12	24
Fabric #5, Plain Blocks—Piece J			
Cut strips 15 1/2" x width of fabric	1	1	3
☐ Crosscut into 15 1/2" squares	1	2	6
Fabric #5, Setting Triangles—Piece K			
Cut strips 22 1/2" x width of fabric	1	2	3
☐ Crosscut into 22 1/2" squares	1	2	3
⊠ Crosscut diagonally twice into quarter-square triangles	4	8	12
Fabric #5, Corner Triangles—Piece L			
☐ Cut 11 1/2" squares from strips used for **Piece K**	2	2	2
◺ Crosscut diagonally once into half-square triangles	4	4	4
Fabric #5, Top & Bottom Inner Border—Twin Size			
Cut strips 2 5/8" x width of fabric		3	
Fabric #5, Top & Bottom Inner Border—Queen Size			
Cut strips 4 3/4" x width of fabric			4
Fabric #5, Side Borders—Queen Size			
Cut strips 2 5/8" x width of fabric			5
Outer Border			
Cut strips 6" x width of fabric	6	7	10
Binding			
Cut strips 2 1/4" x width of fabric	7	8	10

For blocks like Tree of Paradise, make a color key and keep it handy for reference while cutting and piecing.

Piecing Directions

1 Sew **Piece B** to **Piece E**. Make **220(310,550)**. Press seams open. Trim. Set aside **100(130,190)** for the border.

Use 1 1/2" finished triangle paper to make the half-square triangles.

Unit 1

2 Sew a **Piece E** and 3 **Unit 1**s together as shown. Make **4(6,12)**. Press seams open.

Unit 1   Unit 1   Unit 1   Row 1

For precise points, always stitch directly through the intersecting seams of a triangle point, even if the seam allowance will not be exactly 1/4".

3 Sew a **Piece E** and 4 **Unit 1**s together as shown. Make **4(6,12)**. Press seams open.

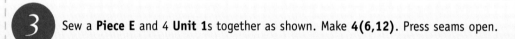

Unit 1   Unit 1   Unit 1   Unit 1   Row 2

4 Sew a **Piece E** and 5 **Unit 1**s together as shown. Make **4(6,12)**. Press seams open.

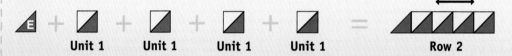

Unit 1   Unit 1   Unit 1   Unit 1   Unit 1   Row 3

Handle **Piece E** and **Unit 1** carefully because of the bias edges.

5 Sew **Rows 1, 2** and **3** together as shown. Make **4(6,12)**. Press seams open.

Row 1

Row 2

Row 3

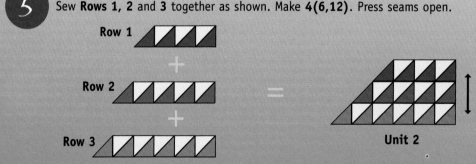

Unit 2

6 Sew **Piece C**, 5 **Unit 1**s and a **Piece E** as shown. Make **4(6,12)**. Press seams open.

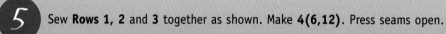

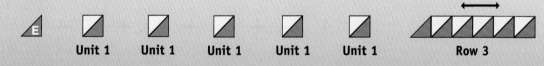

C   Unit 1   Unit 1   Unit 1   Unit 1   Unit 1   E   Row 4

 Sew 1 **Unit 1**, **Piece C**, 5 **Unit 1**s and a **Piece E** together as shown. Make **4(6,12)**. Press seams open.

Unit 1
turned   Unit 1   Unit 1   Unit 1   Unit 1   Unit 1   Row 5

 Sew 2 **Unit 1**s, **Piece C**, 5 **Unit 1**s and a **Piece E** together as shown. Make **4(6,12)**. Press seams open. Remaining **Piece E**s will be used in the border units.

Unit 1   Unit 1   Unit 1   Unit 1   Unit 1   Unit 1   Unit 1   Row 6
turned   turned

 Sew **Rows 4, 5** and **6** together as shown. Make **4(6,12)**. Press seams open.

Row 4

Row 5

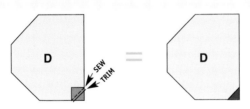

Row 6

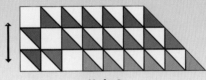

Unit 3

 A. Draw a diagonal line on the wrong side of all **Piece H**s.

B. Place **Piece H**s on the lower right corner of **Piece D** as shown. Sew on the pencil line. Trim seam allowances to 1/4". Make **4(6,12)**. Press.

C. Place **Piece H**s on the lower left corner of **Piece Dr** as shown. Sew on the pencil line. Trim seam allowances to 1/4". Make **4(6,12)**. Press.

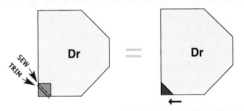

H

D   SEW TRIM   =   D   SEW TRIM   Dr   =   Dr

 Sew Piece D and Piece Dr to opposite sides of Piece G as shown. Make **4 (6, 12).** Press.

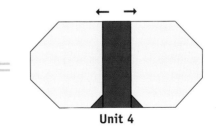

D   +   G   +   Dr   =

Unit 4

Piecing Directions

12 Sew **Piece F** and **Piece I** to **Unit 4**. Make **4(6,12)**. Press.

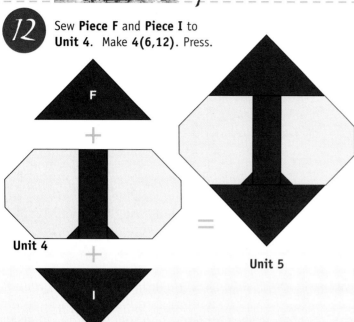

13 Sew **Unit 2** to **Unit 5** as shown. Make **4(6,12)**. Press.

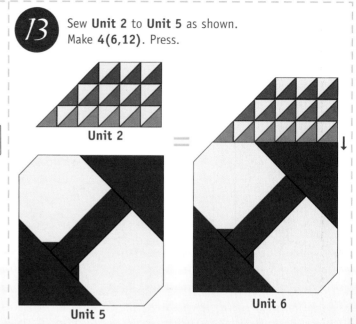

14 Sew **Unit 3** to **Unit 6** as shown. Make **4(6,12)**. Press.

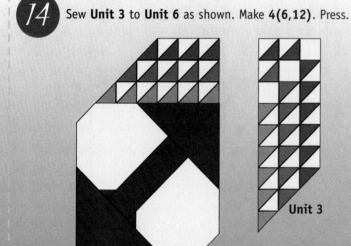

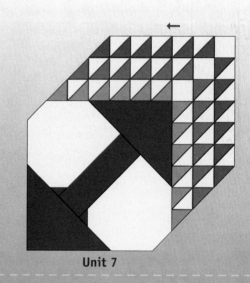

15 Sew **Piece A**s to **Unit 7** as shown. Make **4(6,12)**. Press.

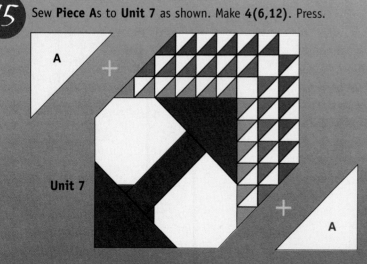

Tree of Paradise Block

Instructions for Pieced Border

1 Sew a **Piece E** to 2 **Unit 1**s as shown. Make **20(26,38)**. Press seams open.

E + Unit 1 + Unit 1 = Unit 8

2 Sew **Unit 8** to the left side of **Piece M** as shown. Make **20(26,38)**. Press.

Unit 8 + M = Unit 9

3 Sew 3 **Unit 1**s and **Piece E** together as shown. Make **20(26,38)**. Press seams open.

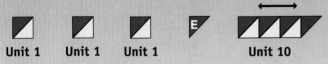

Unit 1   Unit 1   Unit 1   E   Unit 10

4 Sew **Unit 10** to the top of **Unit 9**. Make **20(26,38)**. Press.

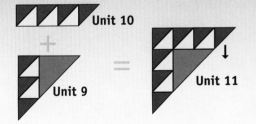

Unit 10 + Unit 9 = Unit 11

Tree of Paradise

Autumn Trees of Paradise, 59" x 59"
5 pieced 15" blocks, 2 plain borders, 1 checkerboard border

Joanne Larsen Line, Duluth, MN
quilted by Angela Haworth, Superior, WI

Joanne chose autumn colors because it is her favorite time of year in northern Minnesota. The quilt is loaded with imagery as Angie machine quilted symbols of fertility and bountiful harvests into her quilting design. A pair of birds grace the center of the outer borders with their tails developing into giant fern fronds.

5 To make the top and bottom borders sew **6(6,9) Piece A**s and **5(5,8) Unit 11**s together as shown. Press seams open.

A   Unit 11   Unit 11   Unit 11   Unit 11   Unit 11

Top and Bottom Border

6 To make the side borders sew **6(9,12) Piece A**s and **5(8,11) Unit 11**s together as shown. Press seams open.

Start and stop sewing the borders exactly 1/4" from the edge of the quilt, backstitching 2 stitches at each end. Sew the top and side borders together and the bottom and side borders together. The corners will be perfectly mitered.

Quilt Assembly

- For precision intersections, butt and pin all seams before sewing.
- Place blocks on design wall and add setting triangle and corners.
- Sew rows together on the diagonal. Press.
- Add background border to the top and bottom edges of the twin-size quilt. Add background borders to the top, bottom, and side edges of the queen-size quilt.

Finishing the Quilt

- Follow the instructions on page 137 for making the quilt sandwich.
- Follow the instructions on page 137 for basting the quilt.
- See page 137 for information on quilting.
- Follow the instructions on page 138 for binding the quilt.

Storm at Sea

Sail On! Sail On!, 50" x 62"
12" blocks (12), 3 borders

Joanne Larsen Line, Duluth, MN
quilted by Karen McTavish, Duluth, MN

Storm at Sea

Brackman/BlockBase Number: 2188a

Earliest publication date: Prior to 1895

(Ladies' Art Company #135)

Storm at Sea is a very old pattern that was in print in the 1895 Ladies' Art Company. H. M. Brockstedt of St. Louis is credited with the founding of this first mail-order quilt pattern company. An 1895 ad mentions 272 patterns, and Storm at Sea was one of them. The pattern was later published by Carrie Hall and Rose Kretsinger in *The Romance of the Patchwork Quilt in America*. Caxton Printers of Caldwell, Idaho, printed the book in 1935.

The Storm at Sea pattern provides an opportunity to create interesting secondary and tertiary designs. There are many versions of the pattern, but this one represents the pattern Gail de Marcken used to illustrate *The Quiltmaker's Gift*. Two of the examples are done in fabrics that are reminiscent of water. The third quilt is done in batiks which gives it a very different look.

This is Joanne's first Storm at Sea quilt, and it will not be her last. She loves the way the colors flow across the quilt. Karen added to the movement of the waves by doing trapunto quilting in the dark blue areas. Karen is famous for her use of trapunto in her quilting designs.

Artist's Secrets

I love this pattern, which illustrates the idea of sewing the ocean's blues into a quilt. It gives a feeling of motion and curves using only triangles. Don't you like the idea of the old Quiltmaker setting up the old sewing machine just anywhere and whipping up the elements into a quilt?

Quiltmaker's Design Challenges

◆ Choose a color palette that reminds you of your favorite lake.

◆ Try an unusual color palette, such as Vicki did, giving her quilt a totally different look.

◆ Combine many fabrics of blues, lavenders, and teals to make your Storm at Sea unique.

◆ Use scraps to make your quilt. Pay attention to value rather than color.

◆ Create the illusion of waves by using trapunto quilting.

◆ Create a special border using one of the block elements.

◆ The Storm at Sea block is an optical illusion block. Experiment with transparencies to enhance the illusion.

A cold, fierce wind was blowing . . .

83

Quilt Information (finished size measurements)

	LAP	TWIN	QUEEN
Quilt Size without Borders	36" x 48"	60" x 84"	84" x 96"
Quilt Size with Borders	50" x 62"	74" x 98"	98" x 110"
Block Size	12"	12"	12"
Number of Blocks	12	35	56
Block Layout	3 x 4	5 x 7	7 x 8
Backing Layout			

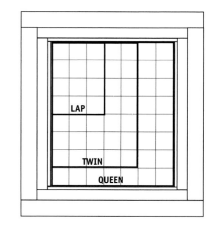

Fabric Requirements (42" wide, in yards)

	LAP	TWIN	QUEEN
Fabric #1, Background—Pieces B, C, F & H	1 1/2	3 1/3	5 1/4
Fabric #2, Aqua—Pieces A, D, E & G	3/4	1 1/2	2 1/4
Fabric #3, Teal—Pieces A, D & I	7/8	1 7/8	2 7/8
Fabric #4, Medium Blue—Pieces A & G	3/8	3/4	1 1/8
Fabric #5, Navy—Pieces A, D & I	7/8	1 7/8	2 7/8
Fabric #6, Purple—Piece A	1/8	1/3	1/2
Inner Border	1/3	1/2	5/8
Middle Border	1/2	3/4	7/8
Outer Border	1	1 3/8	1 1/2
Binding	1/2	2/3	7/8
Backing Fabric	3 1/8	5 7/8	7 1/4

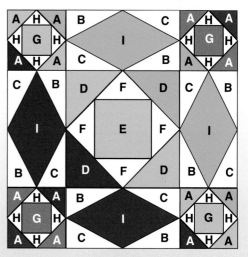

Storm at Sea Block
#2188a

Cutting Instructions continued

	LAP	TWIN	QUEEN
Fabric #1, Background—Piece B			
Cut strips 2 1/8" x width of fabric	6	16	25
With right side of fabric down, trace template B on page 143 to the wrong side of fabric			
Cut on tracing line using a ruler	96	280	448
Fabric #1, Background—Piece C			
Cut strips 2 1/8" x width of fabric	6	16	25
With right side of fabric down, trace template C on page 143 to the wrong side of fabric			
Cut on tracing line using a ruler	96	280	448
Fabric #1, Background—Piece F			
Cut strips 4 1/4" x width of fabric	2	4	7
☐ Crosscut into 4 1/4" squares	12	35	56
☒ Crosscut diagonally twice into quarter-square triangles	48	140	224

Fabric #1, Background—Piece H			
Cut strips 2 3/4" x width of fabric	4	10	15
☐ Crosscut into 2 3/4" squares	48	140	224
☒ Crosscut diagonally twice into quarter-square triangles	192	560	896
Fabric #2, Aqua—Piece A			
Cut strips 2 3/8" x width of fabric	2	5	7
☐ Crosscut into 2 3/8" squares	24	70	112
☑ Crosscut diagonally once into half-square triangles	48	140	224
Fabric #2, Aqua—Piece D			
Cut strips 3 7/8" x width of fabric	2	4	6
☐ Crosscut into 3 7/8" squares	12	35	56
☑ Crosscut diagonally once into half-square triangles	24	70	112
Fabric #2, Aqua—Piece E			
Cut strips 3 1/2" x width of fabric	1	3	5
☐ Crosscut into 3 1/2" squares	12	35	56
Fabric #2, Aqua—Piece G			
Cut strips 2" x width of fabric	2	4	6
☐ Crosscut into 2" squares	24	70	112
Fabric #3, Teal—Piece A			
Cut strips 2 3/8" x width of fabric	2	4	6
☐ Crosscut into 2 3/8" squares	18	53	84
☑ Crosscut diagonally once into half-square triangles	36	105	168
Fabric #3, Teal—Piece D			
Cut strips 3 7/8" x width of fabric	1	2	3
☐ Crosscut into 3 7/8" squares	6	18	28
☑ Crosscut diagonally once into half-square triangles	12	35	56
Fabric #3, Teal—Piece I			
Cut strips 3 1/2" x width of fabric	4	12	19
With right sides of fabric together, trace template I to the wrong side of fabric			
Cut on tracing line using a ruler	24	70	112
Fabric #4, Medium Blue—Piece A			
Cut strips 2 3/8" x width of fabric	2	5	7
☐ Crosscut into 2 3/8" squares	24	70	112
☑ Crosscut diagonally once into half-square triangles	48	140	224
Fabric #4, Medium Blue—Piece G			
Cut strips 2" x width of fabric	2	4	6
☐ Crosscut into 2" squares	24	70	112
Fabric #5, Navy—Piece A			
Cut strips 2 3/8" x width of fabric	2	4	6
☐ Crosscut into 2 3/8" squares	18	53	84
☑ Crosscut diagonally once into half-square triangles	36	105	168
Fabric #5, Navy—Piece D			
Cut strips 3 7/8" x width of fabric	1	2	3
☐ Crosscut into 3 7/8" squares	6	18	28
☑ Crosscut diagonally once into half-square triangles	12	35	56
Fabric #5, Navy—Piece I			
Cut strips 3 1/2" x width of fabric	4	12	19
With right sides of fabric together, trace template I to the wrong side of fabric			
Cut on tracing line using a ruler	24	70	112

For blocks like Storm at Sea, make a color key and keep it handy for reference while cutting and piecing.

Storm at Sea

Waves Along the Lake Walk, 50" x 62" 12" blocks (12), 3 borders

Vicki Fosnacht, Duluth, MN quilted by Quilting Up North, Two Harbors, MN

Vicki recently moved to this area from Indiana and immediately became involved with the Soup Group and North Country Quilters. She is not only a fine quilter, but she also makes beautiful baskets. Merry and Rosemary of Quilting Up North did the interesting quilting design on Vicki's unusual interpretation of Storm at Sea.

Cutting Instructions *continued*

	LAP	TWIN	QUEEN
Fabric #6, Purple—Piece A			
Cut strips 2 3/8" x width of fabric	1	3	4
☐ Crosscut into 2 3/8" squares	12	35	56
☑ Crosscut diagonally once into half-square triangles	24	70	112
Inner Border			
Cut strips 1 1/2" x width of fabric	5	8	9
Middle Border			
Cut strips 2 1/2" x width of fabric	5	8	10
Outer Border			
Cut strips 4 1/2" x width of fabric	6	9	10
Binding			
Cut strips 2 1/4" x width of fabric	6	9	11

Piecing Directions for Corner Blocks

1 Sew **Piece H (background)** to opposite sides of **Piece G (aqua)** as shown. Make **24(70,112)**. Press. Trim dog-ears.

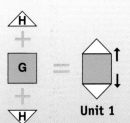

Unit 1

2 Sew **Piece H (background)** to opposite sides of **Unit 1** as shown. Make **24(70,112)**. Press. Trim dog-ears.

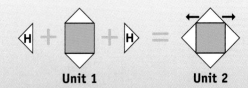

Unit 1   **Unit 2**

3 Sew **Piece A (aqua)** to opposite sides of **Unit 2** as shown. Make **24(70,112)**. Press. Trim dog-ears.

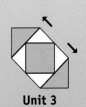

Unit 2   **Unit 3**

4 Sew **Piece A (teal)** and **Piece A (navy)** to opposite sides of **Unit 3** as shown. Make **24(70,112)**. Press. Trim dog-ears.

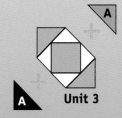

Unit 3   **Unit 4**

5 Sew **Piece H (background)** to opposite sides of **Piece G (medium blue)** as shown. Make **24(70,112)**. Press. Trim dog-ears.

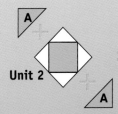

Unit 5

6 Sew **Piece H (background)** to opposite sides of **Unit 5** as shown. Make **24(70,112)**. Press. Trim dog-ears.

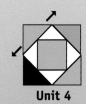

Unit 5   **Unit 6**

For precise points, always stitch directly through the intersecting seams of a triangle point, even if the seam allowance will not be exactly 1/4".

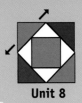

7 Sew **Piece A (medium blue)** to opposite sides of **Unit 6** as shown. Make **24(70,112)**. Press. Trim dog-ears.

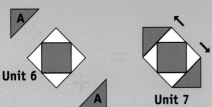

8 Sew **Piece A (navy)** and **Piece A (purple)** to opposite sides of **Unit 7** as shown. Make **12(35,56)**. Press. Trim dog-ears.

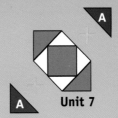

9 Sew **Piece A (teal)** to one side of remaining **Unit 7**s and **Piece A (purple)** to the other side as shown. Make **12(35,56)**. Press. Trim dog-ears.

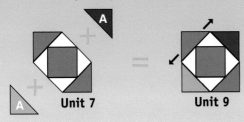

Piecing Directions for Center Block

10 Sew **Piece F (background)** to opposite sides of **Piece E (aqua)** as shown. Make **12(35,56)**. Press.

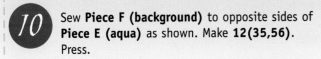

11 Sew **Piece F (background)** to opposite sides of **Unit 10** as shown. Make **12(35,56)**. Press. Trim dog-ears.

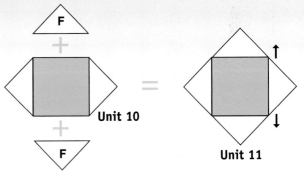

12 Sew **Piece D (aqua)** to opposite sides of **Unit 11** as shown. Make **12(35,56)**. Press.

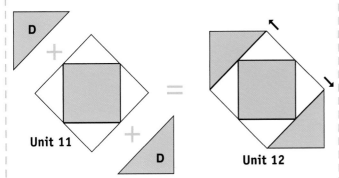

13 Sew **Piece D (teal)** to one side and **Piece D (navy)** to the other side of **Unit 12** as shown. Make **12(35,56)**. Press. Trim dog-ears.

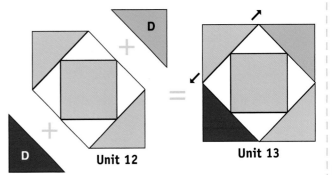

Piecing Directions for Rectangles

14 Sew **Piece B (background)** to opposite sides of **Piece I (teal)** as shown. Make **24(70,112)**. Press.

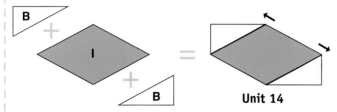

15 Sew **Piece C (background)** to opposite sides of **Unit 14** as shown. Make **24(70,112)**. Press. Trim dog-ears.

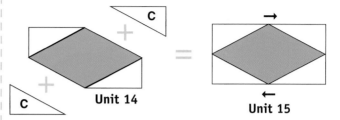

16 Sew **Piece B (background)** to opposite sides of **Piece I (navy)** as shown. Make **24(70,112)**. Press.

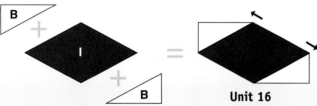

17 Sew **Piece C (background)** to opposite sides of **Unit 16** as shown. Make **24(70,112)**. Press. Trim dog-ears.

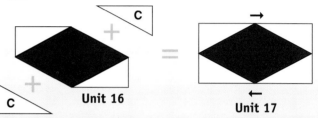

Piecing Directions for Making the Rows

18 Sew **Unit 4**, **Unit 15** and **Unit 9** together as shown to make **Row 1**. Make **12(35,56)**. Press.

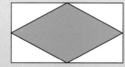

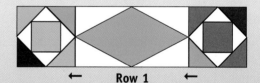

19 Sew **Unit 17**, **Unit 13** and **Unit 15** together as shown to make **Row 2**. Make **12(35,56)**. Press.

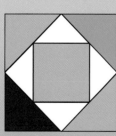

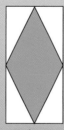

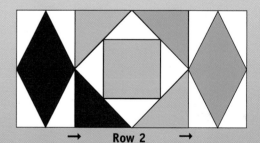

20 Sew **Unit 8**, **Unit 17** and **Unit 4** together as shown to make **Row 3**. Make **12(35,56)**. Press.

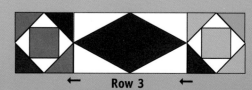

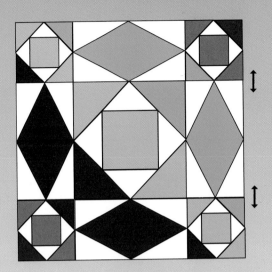

21 Sew **Rows 1, 2** and **3** together as shown. Make **12(35,56)**. Press seams open.

Row 1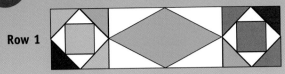

Row 2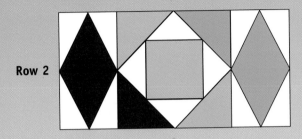

+

Row 3

Storm at Sea Block

Storm at Sea

Chub Lake's Storm at Sea, 50" x 62"
12" blocks (12), 3 borders
Kim Matteen Orlowski, Carlton, MN
quilted by Pam Stolan, Duluth, MN

Kim, who is a program director for a mental health organization, chose traditional blue to make her Storm at Sea. Pam worked nautical knots into the quilting design to give the quilt a feel of the sea.

Quilt Assembly

◆ Lay out the blocks **3(5,7)** across and **4(7,8)** down. The seams have been opened, so blocks should go together nicely.

◆ Before sewing, butt and pin intersecting seams.

◆ Follow the instructions on pages 134 and 135 for sewing blocks and rows together.

◆ Follow the directions on page 136 for adding borders.

Finishing the Quilt

◆ Follow the instructions on page 137 for making the quilt sandwich.

◆ Follow the instructions on page 137 for basting the quilt.

◆ Refer to page 137 for information on quilting.

◆ Follow the instructions on page 138 for binding the quilt.

King's Crown

King Tut's Royal Crown, 51 1/2" x 64"
12 1/2" blocks (12), 3 borders

Diane Nyman, Proctor, MN
quilted by Pam Stolan, Duluth, MN

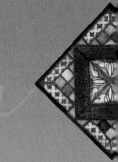

King's Crown

Brackman/BlockBase Number: 3184
Earliest publication date: 1898
(Ladies Art Company #362)
Alternate name: King's Cross,
Old King Cole's Crown, John's Favorite

It has been said that the King's Crown pattern originated in honor of Napoleon. We know that in a 1906 catalog detailing quilting patterns available, the Ladies' Art Company listed King's Crown. There are seven variations of this pattern detailed in The Electric Quilt Company Block-Base computer program, and the variations are each unique. This book stays true to the fourth variation. The construction of this block introduces a technique that may be challenging to less experienced quilters—mitering. Even beginners can perfect the mitering technique if they follow the diagrams and instructions.

Two of the quilts shown are wall hangings, and the featured quilt is a lap size. One of quilts is done in regal-looking fabrics; one is done in jewel-tone colors; and the third has a definite masculine look. One of the quilts shown is set on point, which allows for a large amount of space to highlight the machine quilting. If you look closely, giant moth motifs are visible.

Artist's Secrets

It was the shiny head of the man who was my model for the king that first attracted me to this pattern. Later I realized that a king must wear a crown. So I had him lose his crown a lot and gave him a crown catcher. The jewels are the last things he gives away. The real crown at this point is the great circle dance of joy by his subjects.

Quiltmaker's Design Challenges

◆ To give the quilt an unusual look, try using a border print for Piece E.

◆ Take advantage of the secondary design created by Piece A. Adjust your pattern and color schemes within each block to highlight the secondary pattern that forms among adjacent blocks.

◆ Make a pieced border using either Unit 5 or Unit 6.

◆ Incorporate geometrics to jazz up your quilt.

Diane is a registered nurse and manager of an eye clinic. She maintains her surgical skills by continuing to be involved with eye surgeries. In keeping with the name of the quilt, Diane chose fabrics that give a truly regal look to the final creation. Pam Stolan has had her own quilting machine for several years and incorporates free-motion quilting along with quilting designs developed by others.

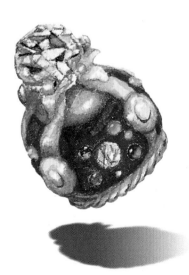

Quilt Information (finished size measurements)

	WALL HANGING	LAP	TWIN
Quilt Size without Borders	25" x 25"	37 1/2" x 50"	62 1/2" x 87 1/2"
Quilt Size with Borders	39" x 39"	51 1/2" x 64"	76 1/2" x 101 1/2"
Finished Block Size	12 1/2"	12 1/2"	12 1/2"
Number of Blocks	4	12	35
Block Layout	2 x 2	3 x 4	5 x 7
Backing Layout	↑	←→ ←→	↓ ↑ ↓

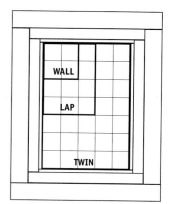

Fabric Requirements (42" wide, in yards)

	WALL HANGING	LAP	TWIN
Fabric #1, Coordinating—Piece A	3/8	7/8	2 1/4
Fabric #2, Background—Piece B & C	3/8	3/4	1 5/8
Fabric #3, Focus—Piece D	1/2	3/4	1 3/4
Fabric #4, Accent—Piece E	1/3	3/4	1 7/8
Fabric #5, Mediums—Piece F	1/4	1/3	3/4
Inner Border	1/4	1/3	1/2
Middle Border	3/8	1/2	3/4
Outside Border	5/8	1	1 1/4
Binding	1/3	1/2	2/3
Backing	1 1/4	3 1/4	6

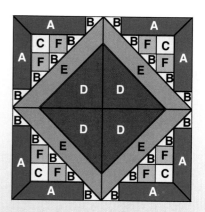

King's Crown Block #3184

For blocks like King's Crown, make a color key and keep it handy for reference while cutting and piecing.

King's Crown

King Heterocea's Crown
12" blocks (4), set on-point, three borders

Joanne Larsen Line, Duluth, MN
quilted by Angela Haworth, Superior, WI

Joanne loves to miter and usually miters all the borders on her quilts. She has a foolproof method for mitering that she shares on page 140. Angie does a lot of research for her original quilting designs. She also did some faux trapunto in the border of this quilt.

Cutting Instructions

	WALL HANGING	LAP	TWIN
Fabric #1, Coordinating—Piece A			
Cut strips 1 3/4" x width of fabric	5	14	40
☐ Crosscut into 1 3/4" x 6" rectangles	32	96	280
▱ With wrong sides together, cut a 45° angle			
Fabric #2, Background—Piece B			
Cut strips 2 1/8" x width of fabric	3	7	19
☐ Crosscut into 2 1/8" squares	40	120	350
◹ Crosscut diagonally once into half-square triangles	80	240	700
Fabric #2, Background—Piece C			
Cut strips 1 3/4" x width of fabric	1	2	6
☐ Crosscut into 1 3/4" squares	16	48	140
Fabric #3, Focus—Piece D			
Cut strips 5 3/8" x width of fabric	2	4	10
☐ Crosscut into 5 3/8" squares	8	24	70
◹ Crosscut diagonally once into half-square triangles	16	48	140
Fabric #4, Accent—Piece E			
Cut strips 1 3/4" x width of fabric	4	12	35
☐ Crosscut into 1 3/4" x 10" rectangles	16	48	140
▱ With wrong sides together, finish cutting with template at right			
Fabric #5, Assorted Mediums — Piece F			
Cut strips 1 3/4" x width of fabric	2	4	12
☐ Crosscut into 1 3/4" squares	32	96	280
Inner Border			
Cut strips 1 1/2" x width of fabric	3	5	8
Middle Border			
Cut strips 2 1/2" x width of fabric	4	5	8
Outer Border			
Cut strips 4 1/2" x width of fabric	4	6	9
Binding			
Cut strips 2 1/4" x width of fabric	4	6	9

**King's Crown
template
Piece E**

King's Crown

Crown Jewels
12 1/2" blocks (4), three mitered borders

Ann Ketcham Palmer, Duluth, MN
quilted by Pam Schaefer, Moose Lake, MN

Ann has quilted for many years and is known for her precision piecing techniques. Ann is a nurse in a local blood bank, and she still remains part of an eye surgery team visiting smaller towns in the area. She has also been part of a medical mission that does eye surgeries in Kingstown on the island of St. Vincent. Pam is a relatively new machine quilter, who enhances a quilt with her creative designs.

Piecing Directions

1 Sew **Piece B** to **Piece A** as shown. Make **16(48,140)**. Press. Trim.

2 Sew **Piece B** to remaining **Piece A**s as shown. Make **16(48,140)**. Press. Trim.

3 Sew **Piece C** to **Piece F** as shown. Make **16(48,140)**. Press.

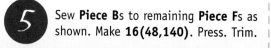

4 Sew **Piece B** to **Unit 3** as shown. Make **16(48,140)**. Press. Trim.

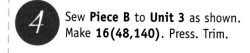

5 Sew **Piece B**s to remaining **Piece F**s as shown. Make **16(48,140)**. Press. Trim.

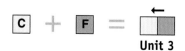

6 Sew **Unit 5** to **Unit 4** as shown. Make **16(48,140)**. Press. Trim.

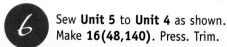

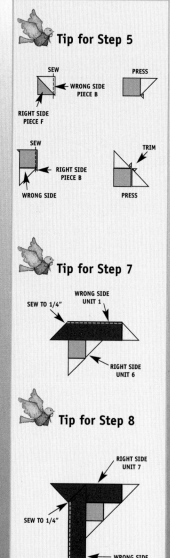

Tip for Step 5

SEW / PRESS / WRONG SIDE PIECE B / RIGHT SIDE PIECE F

SEW / TRIM / RIGHT SIDE PIECE B / WRONG SIDE / PRESS

Tip for Step 7

SEW TO 1/4" / WRONG SIDE UNIT 1 / RIGHT SIDE UNIT 6

Tip for Step 8

RIGHT SIDE UNIT 7 / SEW TO 1/4" / WRONG SIDE UNIT 2

7 Starting 1/4" from the left edge, sew **Unit 1** to **Unit 6** as shown. Make **16(48,140)**. Press.

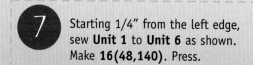
Unit 1
Unit 7
Unit 6

8 Starting 1/4" from the inside edge, sew **Unit 2** to **Unit 7** as shown. Make **16(48,140)**. Press.

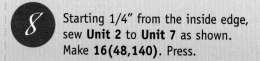
Unit 7
DO NOT SEW MITERED CORNER YET
Unit 8
Unit 2

For precise points, always stitch directly through the intersecting seams of a triangle point, even if the seam allowance will not be exactly 1/4".

9 Fold **Unit 8** in half (**wrong side out**) and sew mitered corners as shown. Start sewing at outside edge and stop sewing 1/4" from inside edge. Make **16(48,140)**. Press seam open. Trim.

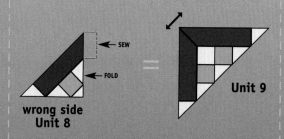
SEW / FOLD / wrong side Unit 8 / Unit 9

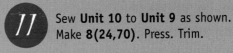

10 Sew **Piece D** to **Piece E**. Make **16(48,140)**. Press **8(24,70)** toward **Piece D** and **8(24,70)** toward **Piece E**.

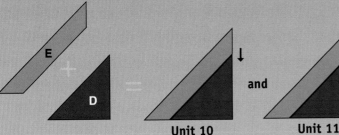

Unit 10   and   Unit 11

11 Sew **Unit 10** to **Unit 9** as shown. Make **8(24,70)**. Press. Trim.

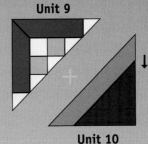
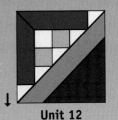

Unit 9

Unit 10   Unit 12

12 Sew **Unit 11** to **Unit 9** as shown. Make **8(24,70)**. Press. Trim.

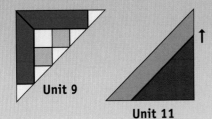
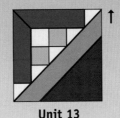

Unit 9

Unit 11   Unit 13

13 Butt and sew **Unit 12** to **Unit 13 (reversed)** as shown. The units will butt perfectly because they were pressed in opposite directions. Make **8(24,70)**. Press.

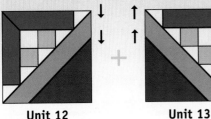
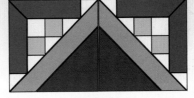

Unit 12   Unit 13 reversed   Unit 14

Quilt Assembly

◆ Lay out the blocks **2(3,5)** across and **2(4,7)** down. For calculating the corner and side setting triangles for the on-point quilt follow the directions on page 135 The plain alternate block in King Heterocea's Crown is the same size as the unfinished pieced blocks, 13".

◆ Follow the instructions on pages 134 and 135 for sewing the blocks and rows together.

◆ Follow the instructions on page 136 for adding the borders.

Finishing the Quilt

◆ Follow the instructions on pages 137–138 for making the quilt sandwich, basting, quilting and binding.

14 Sew two **Unit 14**s together. Make **4(12,35)**. Press.

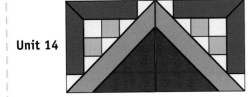

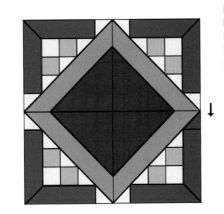

Unit 14

Unit 14 turned

King's Crown Block

Trail of Friendship

Aquatic Trails, 50" x 62"
12" blocks (12), 3 borders

Barbara McKeever, Duluth, MN
quilted by Angela Haworth, Superior, WI

Trail of Friendship

Artist's Secrets

I cheated a bit on this quilt. I love the pattern—drunkard's path—but that name was not appropriate for the children's book. Luckily, there was an alternate name. Note the blue kitten trail of friendship that is following the king as he carries his quilt to the poor.

Trail of Friendship

Brackman/BlockBase Number: 301

Earliest publication date: 1898 (Ladies' Art Company)

Alternate names: Boston Trail, Cleopatra's Puzzle, Drunkard's Trail, Ghost's Walk, Old Maid's Puzzle, King Tut's Crown, Indiana Puzzle, Indiana Pumpkin Vine

The Trail of Friendship block is a variation of the Drunkard's Path block that the Ladies' Art Company published in 1898. This block is a favorite curved pattern and appears as though a bite has been taken out of it. The block is very versatile, twist and turn it and the configuration of blocks produced is endless. The block names are intriguing and enticing. The block was usually done in two colors, a very light and a very dark contrasting color.

During the nineteenth century when the quilt was made in white and blue it was considered to be in support of the temperance movement. The pattern creates a sense of movement throughout the quilt top and is said to suggest an inebriate staggering home after an unruly night out on the town.

Quiltmaker's Design Challenges

◆ Make a Drunkard's Path sampler using a variety of different settings. Suggestions include Dove in the Window, Falling Timbers, Lafayette, Love Ring, Orange Peel, Robbing Peter to Pay Paul. The list is endless.

◆ Set the blocks with alternate plain squares.

◆ For a dramatic look use only two colors. For a scrappy look incorporate as many different fabrics as possible. For a period look consider feed sacks or reproduction fabrics.

◆ Generate a computer design like LaVonne did for her quilt on page 99 She also used the computer to achieve the color paths.

◆ Make a sawtooth border to set off the quilt. Or do a pieced border like Danna did in her quilt on page 98.

◆ This is another block that could be hand pieced. It is small enough to carry with you during your travels or waiting for appointments.

Barb made this stunning quilt using two pieces of batik fabric. Angie quilted it on her commercial sewing machine using bubbles and aquatic pathways.

. . . the king decided to go out into the world and find others who might be in need of his gifts.

97

Quilt Information (finished size measurements)

	LAP	TWIN	QUEEN
Quilt Size without Borders	36" x 48"	60" x 84"	84" x 96"
Quilt Size with Borders	50" x 62"	74" x 98"	98" x 110"
Finished Block Size	12"	12"	12"
Number of Blocks	12	35	56
Block Layout	3 x 4	5 x 7	7 x 8
Backing Layout			

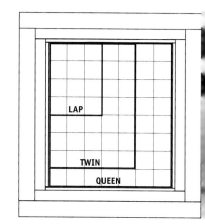

Fabric Requirements (42" wide, in yards)

	LAP	TWIN	QUEEN
Fabric #1, Background—Pieces A & B	1 1/2	3 7/8	5 7/8
Fabric #2, Assorted Batiks—Pieces A & B	1 1/2	3 7/8	5 7/8
Fabric #3, Inner Border	1/3	1/2	5/8
Fabric #4, Middle Border	1/2	3/4	7/8
Fabric #5, Outer Border	1	1 3/8	1 1/2
Binding	1/2	2/3	7/8
Backing	3 1/8	5 7/8	7 1/4

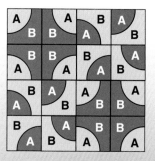

**Trail of Friendship Block
#1039b**

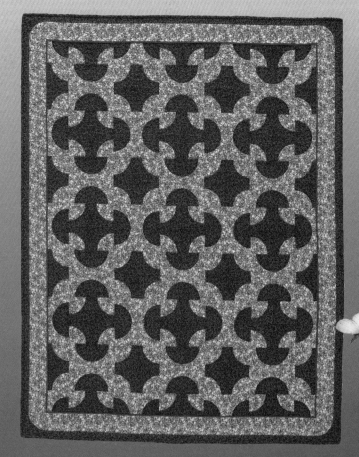

Trail of Friendship

Blueberry Patches Remembered, 46" x 58"
12" blocks (12), two borders

Danna Swenson, Superior, WI
quilted by Sue Kallberg, Solon Springs, WI

Danna used one blueberry fabric but with the color ways reversed. She also used an alternative design, King Tut's Crown for the quilt layout. Note how she used the pattern piece to round the corner on the inner border. Sue did a magnificent job highlighting this unique setting.

Cutting Instructions

	LAP	TWIN	QUEEN
Fabric #1, Background—Piece A			
Cut strips 2 1/2" x width of fabric	6	18	28
☐ Crosscut into 2 1/2" squares	96	280	448
Finish cutting using template on page 101			
Fabric #1, Background—Piece B			
Cut strips 3 1/2" x width of fabric	8	24	38
☐ Crosscut into 3 1/2" squares	96	280	448
Finish cutting using template on page 101			
Fabric #2, Batiks—Piece A			
Cut strips 2 1/2" x width of fabric	6	18	28
☐ Crosscut into 2 1/2" squares	96	280	448
Finish cutting using template on page 101			
Fabric #2, Batiks—Piece B			
Cut strips 3 1/2" x width of fabric	8	24	38
☐ Crosscut into 3 1/2" squares	96	280	448
Finish cutting using template on page 101			
Fabric #3, Inner Border			
Cut strips 1 1/2" x width of fabric	5	8	9
Fabric #4, Middle Border			
Cut strips 2 1/2" x width of fabric	5	8	10
Fabric #5, Outer Border			
Cut strips 4 1/2" x width of fabric	6	9	10
Binding			
Cut strips 2 1/4" x width of fabric	6	9	10

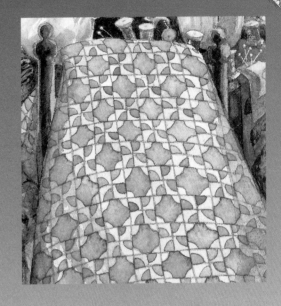

LaVonne's computer-generated quilt layout.

Trail of Friendship

When One Path Ends Another Begins, 67" x 84"
4" blocks (252), three borders

LaVonne Horner, St. Paul, MN
quilted by Carolyn Napper, Beaver Bay, MN

LaVonne always takes a pattern and goes a step beyond. For her Trail of Friendship she generated a computer mockup, hand dyed the fabric, and over dyed the check fabric to achieve this unusual interpretation. She has entered this quilt in several competitions. Carolyn followed LaVonne's pathways with her machine quilting.

Piecing Directions

1 Fold and crease **96(280,448)** batik **Piece A**s as shown. Follow the same process for all background **Piece B**s.

CREASE   CREASE

A   B

2 Lay **Piece B** right side up. Lay **Piece A** right side down on **Piece B** matching crease lines. Place a pin at the exact center using the crease line.

A
B

wrong side Piece A ➞

3 Place a pin at each end of the curved seam as shown.

4 Slowly sew from one end of the curve to the opposite end as shown. It is important to use a scant 1/4" seam allowance. Make **96(280,448)** background **Piece B**s and batik **Piece A**. Press.

5 Sew two **Unit 1**s together as shown. Make **48(140,224)**. Press.

 + =

Unit 1   Unit 1 turned   Unit 2

B + A = ↑

Unit 1

6 Sew **Unit 2** and **Unit 2 reversed** together as shown. Make **24(70,112)**. Press.

Unit 2

+

Unit 2 reversed

= ↑

Unit 3

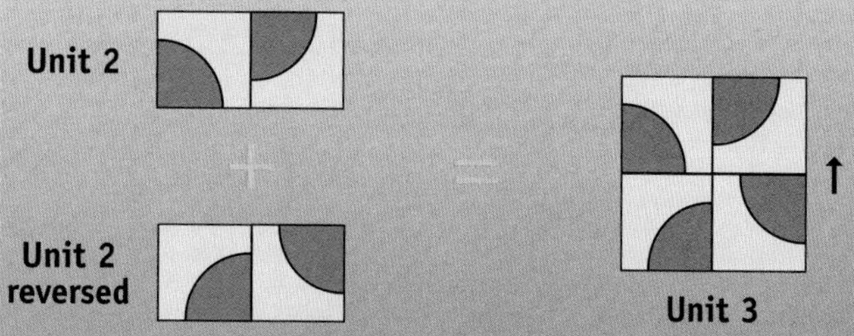

7 Repeat steps 1 through 4, but use the batik **Piece B**s and the background **Piece A**s. Make **96(280,448)** batik **Piece B**s and background **Piece A**s. Press.

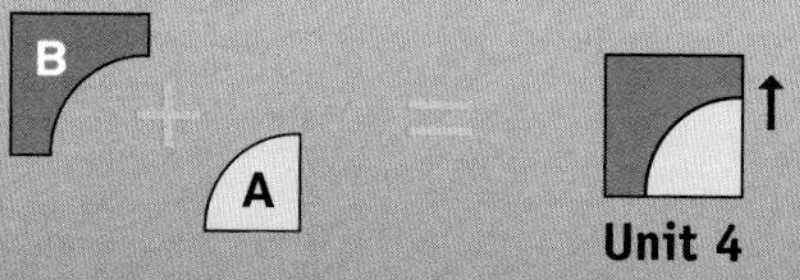

B + A = ↑

Unit 4

8 Sew two **Unit 4**s together as shown. Make **48(140,224)**. Press.

 + =

Unit 4   Unit 4 turned   Unit 5

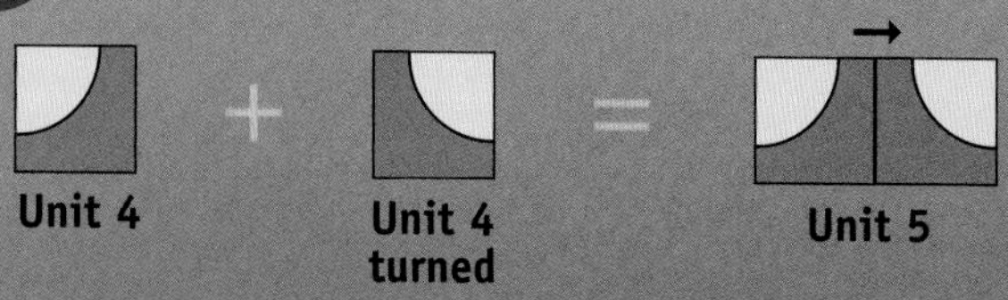

9 Sew **Unit 5** and **Unit 5 reversed** together as shown. Make **24(70,112)**. Press.

Unit 5

+

Unit 5 reversed

= ↓

Unit 6

 For blocks like Trail of Friendship, make a color key and keep it handy for reference while cutting and piecing.

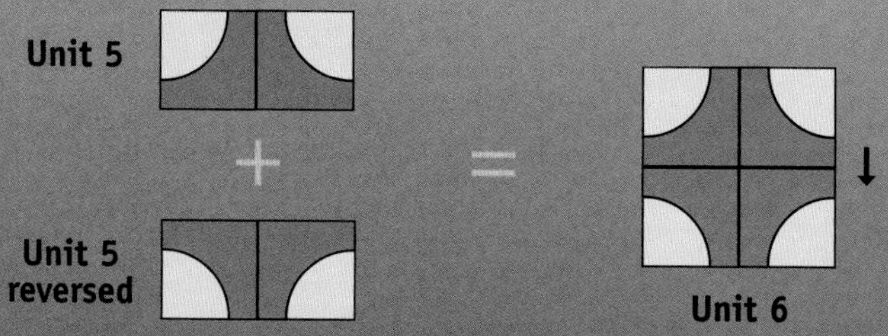

10 Sew **Unit 6** to **Unit 3** as shown. Make **12(35,56)**. Press.

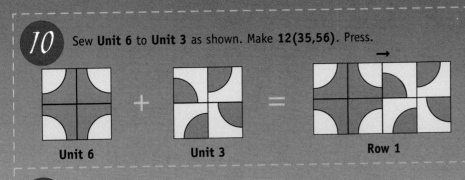

Unit 6   +   Unit 3   =   Row 1

11 Sew **Unit 3** to **Unit 6** as shown. Make **12(35,56)**. Press.

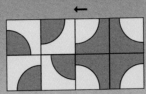

Unit 3   +   Unit 6   =   Row 2

12 Sew **Row 1** to **Row 2** as shown. Make **12(35,56)**. Press.

Row 1

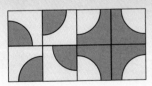
Row 2

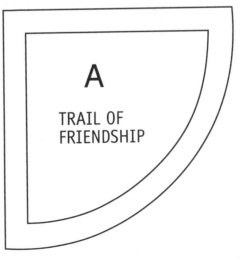
Trail of Friendship Block

Quilt Assembly

Lay out the blocks **3(5,7)** across and **4(7,8)** down.

Sew blocks and rows together following the instructions on pages 134 and 135.

Follow the directions on page 136 for adding borders.

Finishing the Quilt

Follow the instructions on page 137 for making the quilt sandwich.

Follow the instructions on page 137 for basting the quilt.

Refer to page 137 for information on quilting.

Follow the instructions on page 138 for binding the quilt.

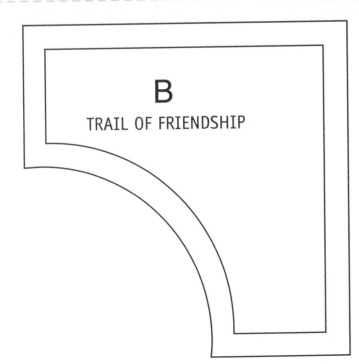

B
TRAIL OF FRIENDSHIP

A
TRAIL OF FRIENDSHIP

Tea Leaf

Joanne's Tea Leaf, 48" x 60"
12" blocks, pieced outer border

Judy Stingl Timm, Duluth, MN
quilted by Sue Kallberg, Solon Springs, WI

Tea Leaf

Artist's Secrets

Since the Quiltmaker so loves drinking tea, and since this pattern is so different from the others, it was an easy choice. The Quiltmaker carries my old teapot throughout the story. I got it our first year of marriage in Singapore and still use it.

Tea Leaf

Brackman/BlockBase Number: 301
Earliest publication date: 1898 (Ladies Art Company #69)
Alternate names: Lafayette Orange Peel, Lover's Knot, Compass, Circle Upon Circle and Bay Leaf

The Tea Leaf block has been around for a very long time. Barbara Brackman, in her book *Encyclopedia of Pieced Quilt Patterns,* writes that the earliest example of this block was *ca.* 1825–60, Shelburne #164. This block was usually hand pieced but has been updated by using machine appliqué and several new rulers designed specifically for this pattern. It is not necessary to purchase the rulers, but they help you to make blocks with exact measurements. Making this block is fun and easy and can become addictive. Two of the quilts are machine appliquéd and machine quilted and one is hand pieced and hand quilted. This pattern is a good way to use up your scraps.

Quiltmaker's Design Challenges

- Try reversing the light and dark fabrics for some of the blocks.
- Sew two pieces of fabric together and cut a leaf template that has a split color combination.
- Use assorted batiks, leaf prints, or novelty prints. Michelle used several Australian fabrics in her quilt.
- Try using William Morris or Liberty of London fabrics for a traditional looking quilt.
- For an unusual look, cut the templates from fabrics that have been string pieced.
- Try hand appliquéing this block. It is a great block to work on while traveling or waiting for an appointment.

. . . with a steaming cup of blackberry tea, she would begin a new quilt.

Judy Timm is a popular teacher at Fabric Works, where she teaches beginning quilting plus many color classes. Joanne came up with the idea to machine appliqué the Tea Leaf, and Judy perfected the technique. Judy is a new grandmother and juggles her time between working and teaching at Fabric Works, designing and making quilts, and spending time with her grandchildren. Sue Kallberg, mother of five, is a bundle of energy.

Quilt Information (finished size measurements)

	LAP	TWIN	QUEEN
Quilt Size without Borders	36" x 48"	60" x 84"	84" x 96"
Quilt Size with Borders	48" x 60"	72" x 96"	96" x 108"
Finished Block Size	12"	12"	12"
Number of Blocks	12	35	56
Block Layout	3 x 4	5 x 7	7 x 8
Backing Layout			

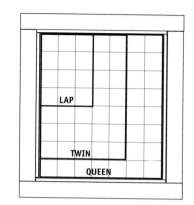

Fabric Requirements (42" wide, in yards)

	LAP	TWIN	QUEEN
Fabric #1, Assorted Backgrounds—Piece A	3 1/4	7 3/4	11 3/4
Fabric #2, Assorted Mediums & Darks—Piece B	2 1/2	5 3/4	8 3/4
Inner Border	3/4	1	1 1/4
Outer Border (fabric included in Fabric #1 and Fabric #2)			
Binding	1/2	2/3	3/4
Backing Fabric	3	5 2/3	7 1/8

Cutting Instructions

	LAP	TWIN	QUEEN
Fabric #1, Assorted Backgrounds—Piece A			
Cut strips 4" x width of fabric	26	67	103
Crosscut into 4" squares	260	668	1,028
Fabric #2, Assorted Mediums & Darks—Piece B			
Cut strips 4 3/4" x width of fabric	17	42	65
☐ Crosscut into 2 1/2" x 4 3/4" rectangles			
Finish cutting using template on page 107	260	668	1,028
Inner Border			
Cut strips 3 1/2" x width of fabric	5	8	10
Pieced Outer Border			
Units made from Fabric #1 and Fabric #2			
Binding			
Cut strips 2 1/4" x width of fabric	6	8	10

Tea Leaf Block
#301

For blocks like Tea Leaf, use a design wall to experiment with color options.

Tea Leaf

Tea at Middlethorpe Park, 43" x 43", 14" blocks, 2 borders

Michele Bowker, Duluth, MN, quilted by Marcia Bowker, Duluth, MN

Second-grade teacher Michelle Bowker received her quilt instructions early on in the design process. The size of the block was later reduced. Michelle made this pattern using mostly Australian fabrics. She was an AFS student in Australia during high school and has many fond memories of the time she spent there. Last year, as part of a science unit, her students made a dinosaur quilt using the iron-on appliqué technique. Her sister Marcia, an occupational therapist specializing in hand rehabilitation, did the machine quilting.

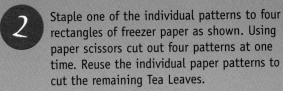

Making the Individual Tea Leaf Units

1 Using the Tea Leaf template on page 143, trace as many patterns as possible onto a piece of 8 1/2" x 11" paper. Cut out the individual patterns.

2 Staple one of the individual patterns to four rectangles of freezer paper as shown. Using paper scissors cut out four patterns at one time. Reuse the individual paper patterns to cut the remaining Tea Leaves.

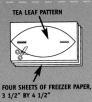

TEA LEAF PATTERN

FOUR SHEETS OF FREEZER PAPER, 3 1/2" BY 4 1/2"

3 Place a freezer paper pattern with the shiny side down on the wrong side of a Piece B. Use a hot, dry iron to press the pattern to the fabric. Use cotton setting on the iron and hold iron on fabric for approximately 10 seconds.

PIECE B WRONG SIDE UP

FREEZER PAPER SHINY SIDE DOWN

4 Using a sharp fabric scissors, cut out the leaf piece adding a 1/4" seam allowance on all sides.

PIECE B WRONG SIDE UP

FREEZER PAPER SHINY SIDE DOWN

Rob's Laser Rulers designed a ruler for the Tea Leaf template.

5 Turn the Leaf pattern over so the shiny side of the freezer paper is up as shown.

PIECE B WRONG SIDE UP

FREEZER PAPER SHINY SIDE UP

6 Carefully iron seam allowance to the leaf pattern. If necessary, use fabric glue or starch sparingly.

PIECE B RIGHT SIDE UP

PIECE B WRONG SIDE UP

FREEZER PAPER SHINY SIDE UP

Roxanne's Glue Baste It works great. Or spray a small amount of spray starch into a bowl and using a Q-tip, dab a small amount where you need it.

The Clover Mini Iron works well for this step.

7 Center leaf appliqué on background Piece A diagonally as shown. Pin as needed.

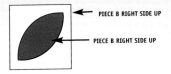

PIECE B RIGHT SIDE UP

PIECE B RIGHT SIDE UP

Rob's Laser Tea Leaf ruler has two lines to help with this step.

8 Thread your machine with .004 nylon monofilament thread on top and a neutral thread in the bobbin. Use a 70/10 universal needle. Set zigzag width to the smallest you can handle. Set stitch length to approximately 1/8".

An open-toe foot makes it easier to see what you are doing.

9 Starting at a gentle curve slowly stitch around the entire leaf pattern. Overlap 2 or 3 stitches to secure.

It will be necessary to stop at the tips of the Tea Leaf with the needle down, and pivot as necessary. Make **260(668,1,028)**. Press.

Place the 45° diagonal line of a 3 1/2" square ruler directly through the center of the block and trim to 3 1/2" as shown. Make sure there is a 1/4" seam allowance on all sides.

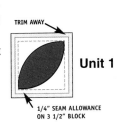

TRIM AWAY

Unit 1

1/4" SEAM ALLOWANCE ON 3 1/2" BLOCK

Rob's Laser Rulers has a 3 1/2" square ruler with two diagonal lines designed specifically for this pattern. The ruler also has the 1/4" seam allowance line clearly marked on all sides.

10 Using a small, sharp fabric scissors, cut a 2" slit in the background fabric directly in the middle of the leaf pattern. Gently remove the freezer paper. If glue was used, fabric must be soaked to soften glue.

Tweezers work great for removing freezer paper.

Piecing Directions

1 Machine appliqué **Piece B** to **Piece A** following directions on page 105. Make **260(668,1028)**. Press. Set aside **68(108,132) Unit 1**s to be used in outer border.

Unit 1

2 Sew two **Unit 1**s together as shown. Make **96(280,448)**. Press seams open.

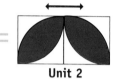

Unit 1 reversed + Unit 1 = Unit 2

3 Sew two **Unit 2**s together as shown. Make **48(140,224)**. Press seams open.

Unit 2

Unit 2 reversed

Unit 3

Use a design wall to help achieve the look you want.

4 Sew two **Unit 3**s together as shown. Make **24(70,112)**. Press seams open.

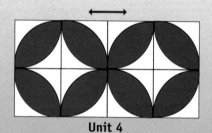

Unit 3 + Unit 3 = Unit 4

5 Sew two **Unit 4**s together as shown. Make **12(35,56)**. Press seams open.

Unit 4

Unit 4 reversed

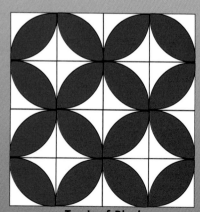

Tea Leaf Block

Quilt Assembly

◆ Lay out the quilt in rows of **3(5,7)** across and **4(7,8)** down.

◆ Experiment with different arrangements of the blocks before deciding on a final placement.

◆ Follow the instructions on pages 134 and 135 for sewing blocks and rows together. Press.

◆ Follow the instructions on page 136 for adding the first border. To make the outside side border, sew 2 rows of **14(22,30) Unit 1**s together as shown in featured quilt. To make the top and bottom border sew 2 rows of **16(24,32) Unit 1**s together. Follow the instructions on page 136 for adding the outside border.

Finishing the Quilt

◆ Follow the instructions on page 137 for making the quilt sandwich.

◆ Follow the instructions on page 137 for basting the quilt.

◆ Refer to page 137 for information on quilting.

◆ Follow the instructions on page 138 for binding the quilt.

TEA LEAF TEMPLATE
B

Above: Awash in making the Tea Leaf quilt.

At right: Auditioning the block layout.

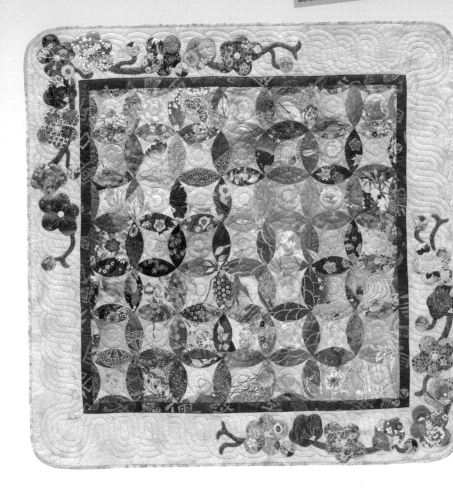

Tea Leaf

Oriental Tea, 40" x 40"
Sandy Thomson, Superior, WI

hand pieced and hand quilted by Sandy Thomson, Superior, WI

Sandy has been teaching hand piecing and hand quilting at Fabric Works ever since the shop opened thirteen years ago. She also teaches color and technique classes, and there is usually a waiting list for all her classes. Sandy prefers to hand quilt and hand appliqué. The beautiful hand appliqué design on the border was taken from Jill Liddell's book Changing Seasons.

107

Grandmother's Flower Garden

Travelin' Granny, 60 3/4" x 64 7/8"
2 1/4" hexagons, 31 full flower blocks,
8 half flower blocks and 54 triad blocks

Toni Gotelaere, Solon Springs, WI
machine and hand quilted
by Toni Gotelaere

Grandmother's Flower Garden

Brackman/BlockBase Number: 160
Earliest publication date: 1835 (*Godey's Lady's Book*)
Alternate names: Honeycomb, Six-sided Patchwork, and Hexagon Patchwork

Grandmother's Flower Garden has long been a favorite of quilters, and the hexagon is considered the most popular shape in English patchwork. The pattern is usually made up of two concentric rows of hexagons around a six-sided center. This pattern features the English paper piecing method for doing the pattern. All three examples are different; the directions are for the featured quilt. Using the English paper piecing method allowed all three quilters to work on their blocks anywhere, any time they had a few spare minutes. The quilt featured uses fussy cut oriental fabrics. One is a memory quilt with blocks made to commerate special occasions such as weddings, births, trips, etc. The third quilt is truly an art quilt that was inspired by the water lily paintings of Claude Monet. All batiks were used, and the hand pieced blocks were machine appliquéd to a large piece of watermarked blue batik.

There are many new products and methods on the market that will speed up the process of making of this classic quilt including acrylic templates in a variety of sizes. One interesting method uses strip piecing, another is a product called Quiltsmart. My favorite is a product from Scrap Magic that has hexagons in three sizes on preprinted freezer paper. The hexagons are reusable and are quick and easy to use.

Quiltmaker's Design Challenges

◆ Consider making a truly scrap Grandmother's Flower Garden paying close attention to value rather than color.

◆ When binding the quilt, think about having the binding follow the edge of each hexagonal patch. Or square off the outside hexagons before binding.

◆ The path row of hexagons could be done in black for a truly dramatic look.

◆ Chose one color family such as a multitude of reds to make the center and petals, and use a red toile for the pathways.

◆ Use registration marks on your fabric to achieve the look Toni did in the quilt on the opposite page.

◆ Mary interpreted a famous Monet painting in her quilt. Consider your favorite artist and try your hand at interpreting his or her work.

Toni got the idea for this layout for her quilt from a quilt made by Gail de Marcken, illustrator of The Quiltmaker's Gift. *Toni is a nurse in the post coronary unit of a local hospital. She made many of the blocks for her quilt during a vacation trip to China. She used registration marks on her fabric to achieve the symmetrical looking flower petals.*

Here and there and wherever the sun warmed the earth, it was said she made the prettiest quilts anyone had ever seen. The greens and purples seemed to come from the abundant wildflowers.

109

Quilt Information (finished size measurements)

LAP		
Quilt Size with Borders 60 3/4" x 64 7/8"		
Backing Layout	↔	
	↔	

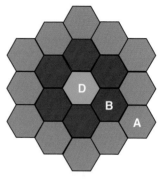

For blocks like Grandmother's Flower Garden, make a color key and keep it handy for reference while cutting and piecing.

Fabric Requirements (42" wide, in yards)

	LAP
Fabric #1, Background—Piece A	2 3/4
Fabric #2, Assorted for Flowers—Piece B & C	1 1/2
Fabric #3, Assorted Centers for Flowers—Piece C & D	3/8
Fabric #4, Triad Filler—Piece E	1 1/4
Fabric #5, Border—Piece F, Binding	2
Backing Fabric	3 7/8

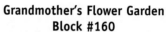

**Grandmother's Flower Garden
Block #160**

Half Flower

Triad Filler

Grandmother's Flower Garden

Hexed No More, 77" x 77"
2 1/4" hexagons, 67 full flower blocks,
6 half flower blocks

Julie Owen, Superior, WI
quilted by Angela Haworth, Superior, WI

Julie does not know who originally made the quilt blocks but does know they have been passed around for over fifty years. She was given the blocks at the North Country Quilters meeting in December of 2001. She brought the quilt to the January 2002 meeting completely quilted. Angie and Julie are good friends and often work on projects together. Angie was only too happy to help Julie finish these long forgotten quilt blocks. The quilt has a new home where it is much appreciated—hence, the title.

110

Cutting Instructions

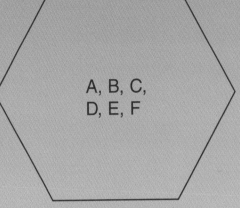

Freezer paper templates	LAP
Cut freezer paper templates totaling	973
Fabric #1, Green Background—Piece A	
Using template at right	
cut fabric 1/4" larger than template on all sides	422
Fabric #2, Assorted Flower Fabrics—Piece B	
Using template at right	
cut fabric 1/4" larger than template on all sides	
For each full flower cut	6
hexagons from the same fabric.	
The total number of sets of 6 needed is	31
Fabric #2, Assorted Flower Fabrics—Piece C	
Using template at right	
cut fabric 1/4" larger than template on all sides	
For each half flower cut	3
hexagons from the same fabric.	
The total number of sets of 3 needed is	8
Fabric #3, Assorted Flower Centers—Piece D	
Using template at right	
cut fabric 1/4" larger than template on all sides	39
Fabric #4, Triad Fillers—Piece E	
Using template at right	
cut fabric 1/4" larger than template on all sides	
For each triad cut	3
hexagons from the same fabric.	
The total number of sets of 3 needed is	54
Fabric #5, Purple Border—Piece F	
Using template at right	
cut fabric 1/4" larger than template on all sides	
Use the same purple fabric and cut hexagons	140
Binding	
Cut strips 2 1/4" x width of fabric	9

A, B, C, D, E, F

Grandmother's Flower Garden template

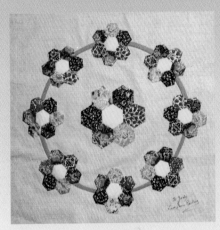

Grandmother's Flower Garden Friendship Wall Hanging
This miniature Grandmother's Flower Garden uses Liberty of London fabric for the flower petals. It is hand pieced and hand appliquéd onto a muslin background. Pauline Grimsby, a friend Judy met during her travels to England made the piece. Judy plans to mat and frame this exquisite piece of work.

Grandmother's Flower Garden

Grandmother's Flower Garden Memories
2 1/4" hexagons, 67 blocks

Judy Beron, Proctor, MN
hand pieced

Judy's memory flower garden is a work in progress. She adds new blocks to commerate special occasions such as the marriages of her children, the birth of a grandchild, anniversaries, a quilting trip to England, or other unique events in her life. She searches out and finds just the right fabric to use for each memory block. Judy's set her blocks with a white pathway, which sets off the blocks beautifully and also makes the quilt larger.

Piecing Directions

The Quiltmaker says . . .

Read all the instructions before you begin.

Always place right sides of fabric together for stitching.

Use scant 1/4" seam allowances.

Press seam allowances in the direction of arrows.

1 Make a plastic template following the directions on page 141 or use a commercial template or other product described in the introduction. Trace and cut **973** freezer paper templates as shown. Place shiny side of freezer paper on the wrong side of the fabric. Press the paper templates to the individual pieces of fabric using a dry iron.

2 Cut 1/4" around all sides of the freezer paper template. This can be done using a ruler and rotary cutter as shown.

3 With the template side up, carefully fold the seam allowance over the paper edge. Use a running stitch to baste the seam allowance, stitching through the paper as shown.

4 To make the full flowers select a set of **6 hexagons** from the same fabric and a coordinating **center hexagon**. With right sides together and folded edges aligned, whipstitch **Piece D** (center) to **Piece B** (flower petal). To whipstitch pull the thread through and reinsert needle in the folds next to the previous stitch, looping thread over the folded edges. To secure the stitches make backstitches or knot the thread at beginning and end. It is important to make tiny stitches and to sew from corner to corner as shown.

Unit 1

Tip for Step 4

PIECE D RIGHT SIDE UP   PIECE B RIGHT SIDE DOWN

5 With right sides together whipstitch another **Piece B** (flower petal) to **Unit 1** as shown. Continue to whipstitch the remaining petals to **Unit 1.**

Unit 1

Unit 2

6 Select **12** green background fabrics and whipstitch them to **Unit 2** as shown. Make a total of **31 Unit 3**s. Press flat.

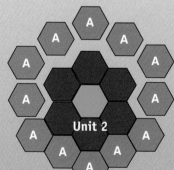

Unit 2

Unit 3

Tip for Step 5

Whipstitch following arrows.

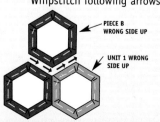

PIECE B WRONG SIDE UP

UNIT 1 WRONG SIDE UP

7 To make the half flowers select a set of **3 hexagons** from the same fabric and a coordinating **center hexagon**. With right sides together whipstitch **Piece D** (center) to **Piece C**s (flower petal) as described in **Step 4.**

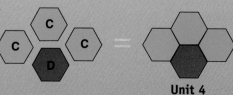

Unit 4

8 Select **5 green background** fabrics and whipstitch to **Unit 4**. Make a total of **8 Unit 5**s. Press flat.

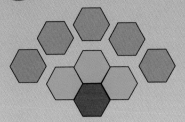

Unit 4

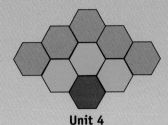

Unit 4

9 Select **3 Triad Filler hexagons** from the same fabric. With right sides together whipstitch the **Piece E**s together as described in **Step 4**. Make **54**. Press.

Unit 4

Quilt Assembly

◆ Lay out the quilt as shown in the featured quilt.

◆ Using a design wall experiment with the placement of the full flowers and the triad units.

◆ Add the purple border hexagons and the ten green background hexagons.

◆ Whipstitch the quilt together. Press flat.

◆ Remove the basting stitches and freezer paper.

Finishing the Quilt

◆ Follow the instructions on pages 137 for making the quilt sandwich.

◆ Follow the instructions on page 137 for basting the quilt.

◆ See page 137 for information on quilting. There is no need to mark the quilt. The featured quilt was machine quilted around the center and the flower petal fabrics. The center fabric and the triad units were hand quilted in various designs enhancing the fabric pattern.

◆ Follow the instructions on page 138 for binding the quilt.

Grandmother's Flower Garden

Nymphéas de Grandmère Monet, 50" x 42"
12 full blocks & 5 partial blocks, two plain borders

Mary Eblom, Duluth, MN
quilted by Angela Haworth, Superior, WI

Mary set out to make a traditional Grandmother's Flower Garden quilt using batik fabrics. Somewhere along the way her muse took over and she made her first art quilt. Inspired by the water lily paintings of Claude Monet she created an award-winning quilt. Angie shared Mary's vision of the quilt and used fifty bobbins of many different types of thread to create the peace and tranquility of the water. Mary who works at Fabric Works in Superior, WI, does 95 percent of her piecing and quilting by hand. Angie uses a commercial sewing machine to do her machine quilting.

Crazy Quilt

Crazy 'bout Quilting, 52" x 66"
12" blocks (12) with pieced border

Diane Knudson, Duluth, MN
embellishments by Diane Knudson

Crazy Quilt

Brackman/BlockBase Number: 2707

Earliest publication date: 1898 (Ladies' Art Company, #219)

Crazy quilting was popular during the Victorian age. The quilts were made with luxurious fabrics such as silks and velvets and used frilly laces, ribbon work, ribbon embroidery, monogramming, and elaborate embroidery stitches to achieve a masterpiece. A Crazy Quilt was made by piecing together irregular shaped pieces of fabric onto a muslin foundation and using creative embroidery stitches to secure the pieces. The pattern below uses the stitch and flip method for keeping the fabrics in place.

The sample Crazy 'bout Quilting was done using two machines. The other example Faux Crazy Quilt is a fast and fun way to do a Crazy Quilt. It was done using the Crazy Quilt fabric designed from the book *The Quiltmaker's Gift*. Each square was embellished with stitches, buttons, mirrors, and other doodads. Sashing was used to set off the blocks. There is also a product called Crazy for You— Foundation by the Yard available to use for making Crazy Quilts.

Each block in the sample starts with a five-sided block. One block has been designed for you and it is suggested you start your quilt using this block as a learning tool. After you have mastered the lesson block, let your imagination soar to create your own unique blocks.

Artist's Secrets

The quilt the Quiltmaker is making for the king is a Crazy Quilt. As the king gives a treasure away, a picture of it is sewn into the quilt. How better to show that one does not need to possess an object to receive joy from it? And that memories are important. Crazy Quilts are wonderful.

Quiltmaker's Design Challenges

◆ Make a quilt using fabrics that have special meaning or memories for you. Use that collection of old silk ties or kimonos that you have been collecting.

◆ Sewing machines have many stitches on them that most people have never tried. Try using as many of these stitches as you can on your Crazy Quilt.

◆ Try creating your own Victorian-era masterpiece by using cottons, velvets, silks, linens, wools, and rayons.

◆ Consider color schemes when designing your quilt. Try a balanced color scheme using equal amounts of darks, lights, and neutral fabrics.

Diane works as a benefits consultant for a local hospital. She enjoys working with fabrics, especially purples. She designs and makes many of her own unique pieces of clothing. This is Diane's first Crazy Quilt. Her sewing machine broke during the process but Kelly J's, a local sewing center, allowed her to come and use their floor model while she waited for hers to be fixed and returned. She later bought the floor model and we are expecting to see many more Crazy Quilts from Diane.

On and on the Quiltmaker worked, and piece by piece the king's quilt grew more beautiful.

Quilt Information (finished size measurements)

	LAP
Quilt Size without Borders	44" x 58"
Quilt Size with Borders	52" x 66"
Finished Block Size	12"
Number of Blocks	12
Block Layout	3 x 4
Backing Layout	← → / ← →

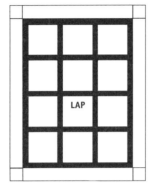

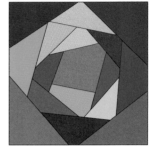

Crazy Quilt Block #2707

Fabric Requirements (42" wide, in yards)

	LAP
Fabric #1, Focus—Piece A	1/2
Fabric #2, 1/2 yard each of 15–16 pieces of subtle prints, Fossil Ferns, Blenders, etc. for a total of	8
Fabric #3, Muslin	2 3/4
Fabric #4, Dark Purple Fabric— for sashing, 1st border, & binding	1 1/3
Backing Fabric	3 1/3
Special Supplies Iron-on stabilizer or freezer paper (yards)	6
Machine embroidery needles, size 90/14 Assortment of specialty threads, i.e., metallic, rayon Sewing machine with a variety of decorative stitches	

Cutting Instructions

	LAP
Fabric #3, Muslin—Block Foundation	
Cut strips 14" x width of fabric	4
☐ Subcut into 14" squares	12
Fabric #3, Muslin—Border Foundation	
Cut strips 6" x width of fabric	6
Fabric #4, Sashing—Piece B	
Cut strips 2 1/2" x width of fabric	3
☐ Subcut into 2 1/2" x 12 1/2" rectangles	8
Fabric #4, Lattice Rows	
Cut strips 2 1/2" x width of fabric	5
☐ Subcut into 2 1/2" x 40 1/2"	5
Fabric #4, Side Lattices	
Cut strips 2 1/2" x width of fabric	3
☐ Subcut into 2 1/2" x 58 1/2"	2
Fabric #4, Binding	
Cut strips 2 1/4" x width of fabric	6

116

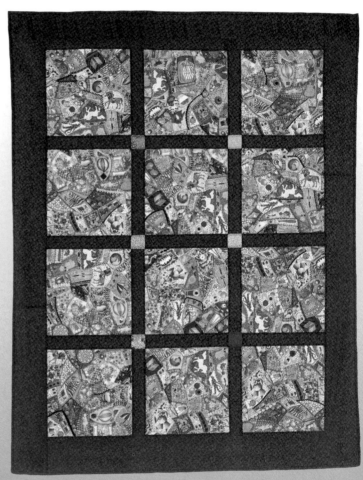

Crazy Quilt

Faux Crazy Quilt, 50" x 63"
12" blocks (12) with sashing and cornerstones, two borders

Brenda Willman, Duluth, MN
embellishments by Brenda Willman, Duluth, MN

Brenda is an army brat, who was born in the Panama Canal Zone, lived all over the world, but knew she found a permanent home the first time she visited Duluth. She started sewing when she was seven years old, making a blouse from a pillowcase. Brenda loves to make kid's quilts and give them away. She has made many Crazy Quilts over the years and has a huge stash of embellishments.

Piecing Directions

1 Draw pattern lines onto the backside of the muslin squares following the suggested pattern designs or design your own. **Make 12**. Number the piecing order on each block as shown. The muslin foundation becomes a permanent part of the block.

2 Start by cutting **Piece A**, the five-sided piece, large enough to cover and overlap **Position #1** by at least 1/4" on all sides as shown below.

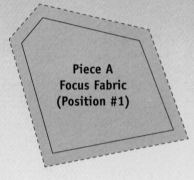

**Piece A
Focus Fabric
(Position #1)**

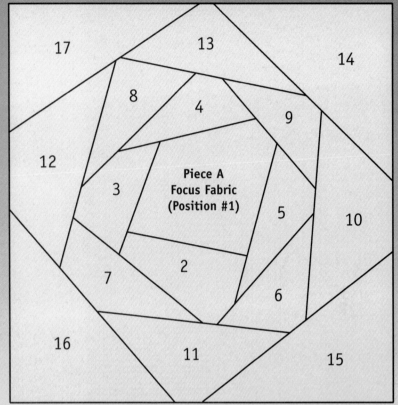

Use the drawing above as your template—at 330 percent it will be 14" square. Or, since the angles are random, use this as an approximation and go crazy!

3 Place **Piece A** right side up in **Position #1** on the unmarked side of the muslin square as shown. Hold foundation up to the light making sure fabric overlaps at least 1/4" on all sides. Place a small pin in the center to hold the piece in place.

4 Cut a piece of fabric for **Position #2** at least 1/4" larger on all sides. Hold foundation up to the light making sure fabric overlaps at least 1/4" on all sides. Lay the second piece of fabric on the first with right sides together.

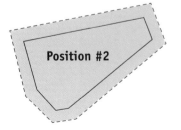

Position #2

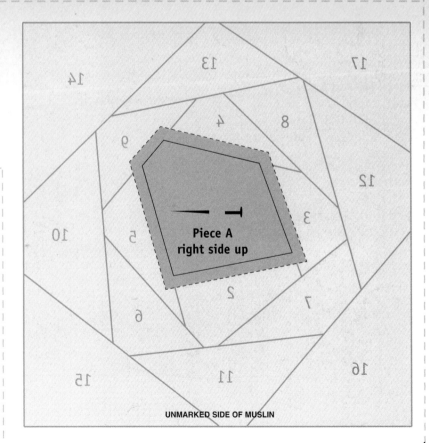

Piecing Directions

5 Using the stitch and flip technique, turn foundation over with marked side facing you and stitch on the line between **Positions #1** and **#2.** Begin and end the stitching one or two stitches beyond the line as shown at right.

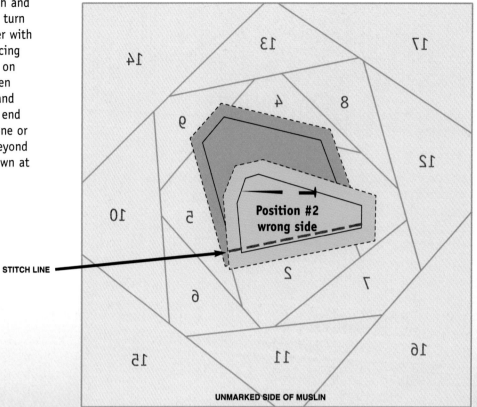

Position #2
wrong side

STITCH LINE

UNMARKED SIDE OF MUSLIN

6 Turn foundation over and trim the two pieces of fabric 1/4" from the sewn line.

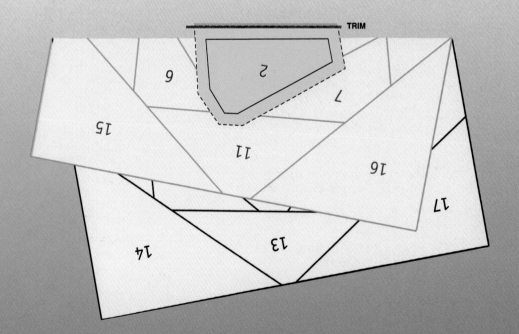

TRIM

118

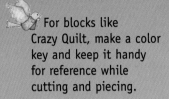

7 Flip **Fabric #2** into place, finger press seam and use a pin or dab of glue to hold piece in place.

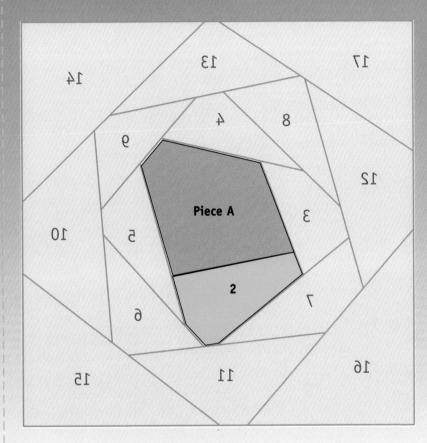

Piece A

Continue to stitch and flip in sequential order until the foundation is completed.

8 Iron freezer paper or iron-on stabilizer to the backside of the muslin squares. This stabilizes the block when doing the embroidery by reducing the stretching of fabric. It also avoids any problems that could be caused by grain lines. The stabilizer will not be removed until the block is completed.

9 Using a variety of stitches embellish all the seam lines, adding embroidery stitches, ribbons, buttons, laces, or whatever pleases your fancy.

10 Trim blocks to 12 1/2". Use a running stitch 1/8" in from the edge on all sides to stabilize the block.

11 Continue the process until you have completed 12 blocks.

For blocks like Crazy Quilt, make a color key and keep it handy for reference while cutting and piecing.

Quilt Assembly

◆ To make a Block Row, use **3 Crazy Quilt Blocks** and **2 Piece B**s. Sew the row together. Make 4 rows. Press.

◆ Starting with a lattice row sew the Lattice Rows to the Block Rows. Press.

◆ Sew the lattice pieces to the sides of the quilt.

◆ To make the pieced border use the 6" x width of fabric muslin fabric. Piece together and cut into outside border strips. It looks best of the pieces are added slightly askew as per the featured quilt. Trim the border piece to 4 1/2" wide.

◆ Make four 6" miniature Crazy Quilt blocks for the corners follow the pattern directions. Trim the blocks to 4 1/2". Add a block to each corner of the top and bottom pieced border.

◆ Follow the instructions on page 136 for adding borders.

Finishing the Quilt

◆ Batting is generally not used in a Crazy Quilt.

◆ Refer to page 137 for information on tying the quilt.

◆ Follow the instructions on page 138 for binding the quilt.

Fish

School's in Session, 45" x 45"
12" blocks (9), 2 plain borders,
1 pieced border

Marsha Wells, St. Cloud, MN
quilted by Kim Wells and
Cindy Provencher, Duluth, MN

Fish

Fish

Brackman/BlockBase number: 3828

Earliest publication date: 1931 (McKim Studios)

Alternate names: An Airplane Motif, Bass & Trout, Gold Fish, Whirligig

Anyone looking at the Fish pattern can clearly see where it gets its name. The Fish pattern was often used in early samplers and was made using two calicos and a background fabric. The original pattern required hand piecing, but the pattern written for this book uses the paper piecing method. By following the paper piecing instructions on pages 117–119 this becomes a relatively easy quilt to make with stunning results.

McKim Studios in Independence, Missouri, was a mail-order source for patterns. Ruby Short McKim also syndicated a newspaper column with full-size patterns in the late 1920s and 1930s. The Fish Block was later reprinted by Dover Publications, Inc., in 1962 in the book *101 Patchwork Patterns*. This is a must-have book if you are interested in quilting history. The book is entertaining and is chock full of facts and the history of quilting written in a humorous and charming manner.

Quiltmaker's Design Challenges

◆ Seek interesting fish fabrics like Joanne used in her wall hanging.

◆ Use bright colors and a black background.

◆ Try doing a scrap quilt using a different fabric for each fish body and fin.

◆ Consider using only two fabrics for the fish body and fin.

◆ This is a great quilt to highlight your collection of unique fabrics.

◆ For an interesting effect, use a scale pattern for the hand or machine quilting.

Next the king fetched . . . the dozen fish that were clear as glass.

Marsha has been quilting for several years. When she saw the Fish pattern, she knew she had to do it. Her mom, Kim, had worked out the pattern for the paper piecing, and she wanted to test it. She used only batiks and added an interesting pieced border of half-square triangles. Kim and Cindy collaborated on the quilting design.

Quilt Information (finished size measurements)

	WALL HANGING	LAP	TWIN
Quilt Size without Borders	36" x 36"	36" x 48"	60" x 84"
Quilt Size with Borders	50" x 50"	50" x 62"	74" x 98"
Finished Block Size	12"	12"	12"
No. of Blocks	9	12	35
Block Layout	3 x 3	3 x 4	5 x 7
Backing Layout			

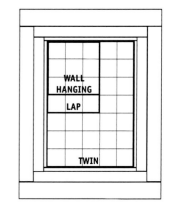

Fabric Requirements (42" wide, in yards)

	WALL HANGING	LAP	TWIN
Fabric #1, Fish Body & Fin—Piece A, B, & G	7/8	1	2 3/8
Fabric #2, Fish Body & Fin—Piece A, B, & G	7/8	1	2 3/8
Fabric #3, Fish Body & Fin—Piece A, B, & G	7/8	1	2 3/8
Fabric #4, Fish Body & Fin—Piece A, B, & G	7/8	1	2 3/8
Fabric #5, Light Background—Piece C, D, & F	1 7/8	2 1/3	6 1/4
Fabric #6, Medium Dark Background—Piece E	1 1/8	1 3/8	3 3/8
Inner Border, Medium Batik	3/8	3/8	1/2
Middle Border, Pieced from Fabric #1–5			
Outer Border, Medium Batik	3/4	1	1 1/3
Binding	1/2	1/2	2/3
Backing	3 1/8	3 1/8	5 1/2

**Fish Block
#3828**

Cutting Instructions

	WALL HANGING	LAP	TWIN
Fabric #1, Fish Body—Piece A			
Cut strips 3 1/2" x width of fabric	3	4	12
Crosscut into 3 1/2" x 7" rectangles	18	24	70
Fabric #1, Fish Fin—Piece B			
Cut strips 3" x width of fabric	3	4	10
Crosscut into 2" x 3" rectangles	36	48	140
Fabric #1, Middle Border—Piece G			
Cut strips 2 7/8" x width of fabric	1	1	2
Crosscut into 2 7/8" squares	10	12	19
Crosscut diagonally once into half-square triangles	20	23	38
Fabric #2, Fish Body—Piece A			
Cut strips 3 1/2" x width of fabric	3	4	12
Crosscut into 3 1/2" x 7" rectangles	18	24	70
Fabric #2, Fish Fin—Piece B			
Cut strips 3" x width of fabric	3	4	10
Crosscut into 2" x 3" rectangles	36	48	140

Cutting Instructions *continued*

	WALL HANGING LAP		TWIN
Fabric #2, Middle Border—Piece G			
Cut strips 2 7/8" x width of fabric	1	1	2
☐ Crosscut into 2 7/8" squares	10	12	19
☑ Crosscut diagonally once into half-square triangles	20	23	38
Fabric #3, Fish Body—Piece A			
Cut strips 3 1/2" x width of fabric	3	4	12
☐ Crosscut into 3 1/2" x 7" rectangles	18	24	70
Fabric #3, Fish Fin—Piece B			
Cut strips 3" x width of fabric	3	4	10
☐ Crosscut into 2" x 3" rectangles	36	48	140
Fabric #3, Middle Border—Piece G			
Cut strips 2 7/8" x width of fabric	1	1	2
☐ Crosscut into 2 7/8" squares	10	12	19
☑ Crosscut diagonally once into half-square triangles	20	23	38
Fabric #4, Fish Body—Piece A			
Cut strips 3 1/2" x width of fabric	3	4	12
☐ Crosscut into 3 1/2" x 7" rectangles	18	24	70
Fabric #4, Fish Fin—Piece B			
Cut strips 3" x width of fabric	3	4	10
☐ Crosscut into 2" x 3" rectangles	36	48	140
Fabric #4, Middle Border—Piece G			
Cut strips 2 7/8" x width of fabric	1	1	2
☐ Crosscut into 2 7/8" squares	10	12	19
☑ Crosscut diagonally once into half-square triangles	20	23	38
Fabric #5, Light Background—Piece C			
Cut strips 2" x width of fabric	9	12	35
☐ Crosscut into 2" x 2 1/2" rectangles	144	192	560
Fabric #5, Light Background—Piece D			
Cut strips 2" x width of fabric	16	22	63
☐ Crosscut into 2" x 4 1/2" rectangles	144	192	560
Fabric #5, Middle Border—Piece F			
Cut strips 2 7/8" x width of fabric	3	4	6
☐ Crosscut into 2 7/8" squares	40	46	76
☑ Crosscut diagonally once into half-square triangles	80	92	152
Fabric #6, Medium Background—Piece E			
Cut strips 4" x width of fabric	8	10	28
☐ Crosscut into 4" squares	72	96	280
Inner Border			
Cut strips 1 1/2" x width of fabric	4	5	8
Outer Border			
Cut strips 4 1/2" x width of fabric	4	5	9
Binding			
Cut strips 2 1/4" x width of fabric	5	6	9

For blocks like Fish, make a color key and keep it handy for reference while cutting and piecing.

Piecing Directions

See page 143 for paper piecing patterns.

1 Paper piece **Unit 1** and **Unit 2** using **Fabric #1** for the fish body and fins. Follow the number sequence listed on the pattern piece. Make **18(24,70)**.

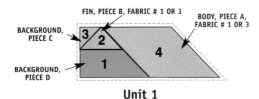

FIN, PIECE B, FABRIC # 1 OR 3
BACKGROUND, PIECE C
BODY, PIECE A, FABRIC # 1 OR 3
BACKGROUND, PIECE D

Unit 1

MEDIUM BACKGROUND, PIECE E
BACKGROUND, PIECE D
BACKGROUND, PIECE C
FIN, PIECE B, FABRIC # 1 OR 3

Unit 2

2 Sew **Unit 1** to the right side of **Unit 2** as shown. Make **18(24,70)**.

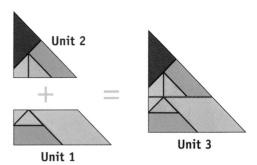

Unit 2 + Unit 1 = **Unit 3**

3 Paper piece **Unit 1 Reversed** and **Unit 2 Reversed** using **Fabric #2** for the fish body and fins. Follow the number sequence listed on the pattern piece. Make **18(24,70)**.

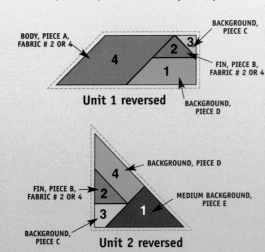

BODY, PIECE A, FABRIC # 2 OR 4
BACKGROUND, PIECE C
FIN, PIECE B, FABRIC # 2 OR 4
Unit 1 reversed
BACKGROUND, PIECE D

BACKGROUND, PIECE D
FIN, PIECE B, FABRIC # 2 OR 4
MEDIUM BACKGROUND, PIECE E
BACKGROUND, PIECE C
Unit 2 reversed

4 Sew **Unit 1 Reversed** to the right side of **Unit 2 Reversed** as shown. Make **18(24,70)**.

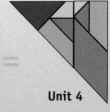
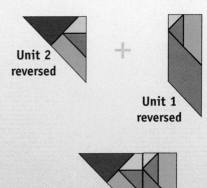

Unit 2 reversed + Unit 1 reversed = **Unit 4**

5 Sew the long side of **Unit 3** and **Unit 4** together as shown. Make **18(24,70)**. Press seams open.

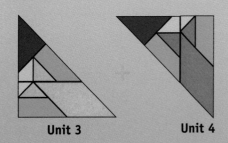

Unit 3

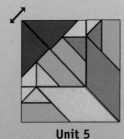

Unit 4

Unit 5

6 Repeat **Step 1** and **Step 2** using **Fabric #3** for the fish body and fins.

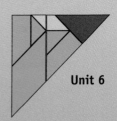

Unit 6

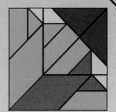

7 Repeat **Step 3** and **Step 4** using **Fabric #4** for the fish body and fins.

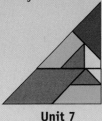

Unit 7

8 Sew the long side of **Unit 6** and **Unit 7** together as shown. Make **18(24,70)**. Press seams open.

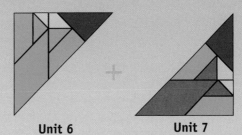

Unit 6 + **Unit 7** = **Unit 8**

9 Sew **Unit 5** to **Unit 8** as shown. Make **18(24,70)**. Press seams open.

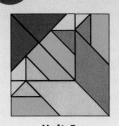 + 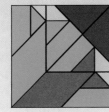 =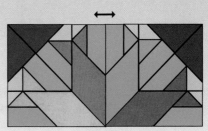

Unit 5 **Unit 8** **Unit 9**

10 Sew **Unit 9** to **Unit 9 reversed** as shown. Make **9(12,35)**. Press seams open.

Unit 9

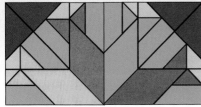

+

Unit 9 reversed

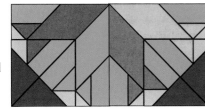

=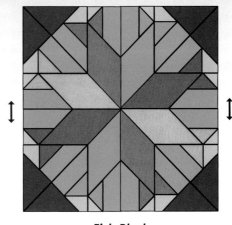

Fish Block

Instructions for Making the Middle Border

1 Sew half-square triangles using **Piece F** of the Background **Fabric #5** and **Piece G** of Fabrics **#1, 2, 3,** and **4.** Make equal amounts of each of the four fabrics for a total of **80(92,152)**. Press.

F + **G** =

Use 2" finished triangle paper to make the half-square triangles.

125

Instructions for making the Middle Border continued

2 Sew the side rows using **19(25,43)** of the half-square triangles. Sew the triangles in color order.

3 Sew the top and bottom rows using **21(21,33)** of the half-square triangles. Sew the triangles in color order.

Quilt Assembly

◆ Lay out the blocks in rows, **3(3,5)** across and **3(4,7)** down.

◆ For precision intersections, butt and pin all seams before sewing.

◆ Sew blocks and rows together following the instructions on pages 134 and 135.

◆ Follow the instructions on page 136 for adding borders.

Finishing the Quilt

◆ Follow the instructions on page 137 for making the quilt sandwich.

◆ Follow the instructions on page 137 for basting the quilt.

◆ Refer to page 137 for information on quilting.

◆ Follow the instructions on page 138 for binding the quilt.

Fish

Swimming Upstream, 22" x 22"
12" block (1), 1 checkerboard border and 2 plain borders

Joanne Larsen Line, Duluth, MN
quilted by Angela Haworth, Superior, WI

Joanne had the wonderful piece of fish fabric in her collection and matched fabrics from Primrose Gradations of Two Harbors, MN, to make the fish and used a dark Aubergine as a background. She made the 1" checkerboard from the leftovers. She added a 1/2" second border and topped off the quilt with the fish fabric. Angie added bubbles to the background piece and did some freehand quilting on the border fish.

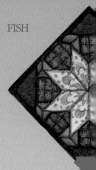

Fish

Star Fish, 50" x 62"
12" blocks (12), 2 borders

Kim Hoffmockel Wells, Duluth, MN
quilted by Kim Wells and Cindy Provencher

Kim designed the paper piecing pattern for the Fish quilt. She is an excellent paper piecer and enjoys the challenges of designing new and interesting patterns. Once again Kim and Cindy worked together to do the machine quilting.

Quilting Basics

Quilting requires having the right tools and equipment to complete a project. Here is a short list of the essential equipment you will need to successfully make one of the quilts in this book. Remember you can always add more tools and gadgets to your collection at a later time.

Iron

A hot steam iron and adjustable-height ironing board with cotton or Teflon cover.

Pins

Fine, sharp, glass headpins are best for most pinning and will not rust. For pin-basting the quilt layers, #2 safety pins work best.

Pin Cushion

A magnetic pin cushion keeps pins handy and helps locate strays.

Rotary Rulers

These clear, acrylic rulers are marked lengthwise, crosswise, and diagonally with easy to read lines and numbers. Buy two rulers to start, a 6" x 24" rectangle and a 6" or 12 1/2" square. Ask for sandpaper discs to put underneath to prevent slippage while cutting.

Keep a wish list of tools to jog your memory when asked what you want for your birthday.

Buy the best equipment, supplies, and materials you can afford. They will last longer and cost less in the long run.

Rotary Mat

Essential companion to the rotary cutter. Buy a self-healing mat that is at least 11" x 17". Both sides can be used for cutting. Beware—these magical mats will warp beyond salvation if left in direct sunlight, a hot car, or below zero temperatures.

Rotary Cutter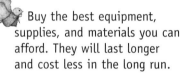

This is the tool that has revolutionized quilting. Buy a medium size (45 mm) straight or ergonomic cutter. Works for left- or right-handers.

Scissors

A small, sharp scissors is needed for snipping threads and trimming dog-ears.

Seam Ripper

Also known as the reverse sewing tool. Keep several sharp ones with fine points on hand for the inevitable undoing of seams.

Sewing Machine

A basic machine that stitches forward and backward will answer all your quilting needs. A special 1/4" presser foot is well worth the investment. Keep your sewing machine clean and in good working order.

Sewing Machine Needles

A size 80/12 needle is an excellent choice for quilting. Change your needle every eight to ten hours or with each new project.

Thread

Use 100 percent cotton thread for machine piecing. A light to medium gray or tan thread will work on most projects.

Invest in the Essential Quilting Tool: An Accurate ¼" Seam

Fabric Works owner, Barb Engelking, reports that inaccurate seam allowances account for 90 percent of the problems quilters have in following patterns.

The patterns in this book call for a scant 1/4" seam allowance (except when piecing quilt backings). Scant means just less than 1/4", to allow for the turn of fabric when the seam is pressed. Sewing a consistent, accurate 1/4" seam allowance is essential for precision piecing.

◆ Cut 3 pieces of scrap fabric 1 1/2" x 3 1/2".

◆ Sew these strips together along the lengthwise edge.

◆ Press the seams away from the center strip.

◆ Measure the sewn unit. It should measure exactly 3 1/2" from edge to edge.

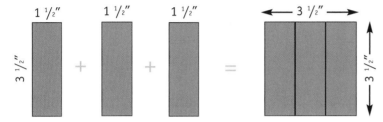

If the sewn unit is NARROWER than 3 1/2", your seam allowance is TOO WIDE.

If the sewn unit is WIDER than 3 1/2", your seam allowance is TOO NARROW.

Make the adjustments necessary to achieve an accurate 1/4" seam allowance every time.

Tips for Making an Accurate 1/4" Seam

◆ Purchase a special 1/4" foot for your machine.

◆ Use a clear ruler to mark a 1/4" line from the throat plate all the way to the front edge of your machine.

Use a permanent marker, masking/duct tape, moleskin, or Post-it notes to mark the line.

◆ The angle at which you feed the fabric under the presser foot helps determine the actual seam allowance. Try to keep fabric straight at 1/4" several inches in front of the needle.

◆ Practice until you can make consistent 1/4" seams.

Design Wall

Several quilts in this book lend themselves to a variety of artistic interpretations before and after the blocks are constructed. The best way to experiment with design options is to play with the pieces or finished blocks on a flat, vertical surface covered with fuzzy fabric (flannel, fleece, felt) that holds the blocks in place without pins, so you can rearrange and reconsider until you find a pleasing effect. Most quilters find a design wall essential to their creative process. We have suggested it in this book for experimenting with blocks like Peace & Plenty, Hither & Yon, and Next-Door Neighbor.

A design wall doesn't have to be fancy. Five yards of white flannel or fleece will make a 90" x 94" portable wall you can pin up when needed and fold away easily for storage—with the quilt pieces still in place if you want! A flannel-back tablecloth also works fine. To make a more permanent installation, nail, tape, staple, or pin flannel to a foam insulation board or sheet of plywood—the bigger the better. Then step back and let your creative juices flow.

Shelly auditions her block layout and borders on a design wall.

The author's stash.

Shari Guimont and Shirley Kirsch audition border fabric at Fabric Works, Superior, WI.

Fabric

Cotton, Cotton, Cotton

Although quilts historically have been made from nearly every kind of fabric (including wools, silks, velvets, feed sacks, shirtings, muslin, sheetings, and recycled fabrics of all kinds), most quilters today prefer 100 percent cotton for its handling properties during construction and sturdiness after completion.

Stay away from polyester and polyester/cotton blends as they are difficult to work with and will not wear evenly with other fabrics in the quilt. Making a quilt requires repeated handling of the fabric, so buy the best quality you can afford.

Choices, Choices, Choices

Choosing fabric for a quilt can be exhilarating or intimidating. What color combination? How many fabrics? Country look or contemporary? Solids or patterns? Florals or calicoes? Brights or pastels?

If you feel unsure about colors or fabrics, try Joanne's recommended strategy below or ask at your local quilt shop. They need your support to stay in business, and the staff will be delighted to help you find fabrics that fit YOUR tastes and your chosen quilt pattern.

Joanne's Fabric Selection Strategy

◆ Choose a fabric that makes your heart sing!

◆ Start with a multicolor focus fabric. Usually this will be a print with three or four color families in a harmonious combination and several variations within each color. See color wheel opposite for the twelve color families.

◆ You may not notice all the colors at first, but look closely to see the various families that are represented. For example, a floral usually has several shades of green and two or more colors of petals plus a background color and some accent color. Novelty prints may have every color under the rainbow.

◆ Select several coordinating fabrics. Don't hurry the process! Choose LOTS of possibilities first, then narrow down your options later.

◆ Start by choosing a light, medium, and dark value fabric from EACH of the color families in your focus fabric.

◆ Among these fabrics, mix and match different color intensity (bright to pastel, clear to grayed), type of pattern (geometric, floral, tone on tone, blender, abstract, pictorial), and scale (tiny, huge, and sizes in between).

◆ Assemble all your choices together on a counter where you can see them interact with the focus fabric and with each other. Step back and evaluate the collection.

◆ You do not need to use all the fabrics. Add and subtract fabrics until you find a combination that will work well in your quilt. Occasionally you may find that your original focus fabric is no longer needed.

◆ Start piecing! Don't be surprised if you find additional fabrics to add along the way. A quilt is a work in process until the final stitch is taken.

Fabric Preparation

Prewash all fabric in warm water with a mild soap to remove excess dye and chemicals. Always wash light and dark fabrics separately.

With dark colors and fabrics that may have unstable color (indigoes, batiks, hand-dyes, bargain fabrics), soak overnight in cold water. If the water discolors, the fabric will bleed. Wash until the water comes clear or do not use the fabric.

Damp dry the fabric on a warm cycle and press with a dry iron.

 For extra body, use spray starch before cutting and piecing.

Grain Lines and Bias

Fabric is woven from perpendicular threads. The crosswise grain tends to stretch a little. The lengthwise grain stretches very little. These two grain lines are often referred to as straight of grain. The selvage (or self-edge), made where the thread turns back on itself at the edge, does not stretch at all and should be trimmed off before measuring and cutting quilt pieces.

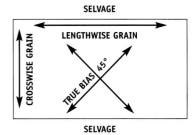

When you cut diagonally across the straight of the grain, you create a bias edge. Bias edges stretch easily and must be handled, sewn, and pressed carefully.

◆ Strips, squares, and rectangles are always cut on the straight of grain.

◆ Shapes such as triangles cannot have all edges cut on-grain. At least one side will be on the bias. To stabilize seams, most patterns try to sew the bias edge of a triangle to a straight edge of the adjacent piece.

◆ Be careful not to stretch bias edges. Do not press bias edges until after they are stitched.

Barb McKeever and Judy Timm check out the novelty fabrics.

Judy Timm arranges fabric. The quilt in the background is an original design by Claudia Clark Myer and shop owner, Barb Engelking.

Color Harmony

Color harmony refers to the pleasing choice, proportion, and arrangement of colors. Although our response to color is usually quite personal, there are several color harmonies that most people find pleasing, and the basic principles are quite simple. Using the color wheel developed by Danish artist Johannes Itten, even beginners can choose color harmonies with confidence.

Experiment with the five basic color schemes and variations shown here. As you consider fabric choices, try to keep an open mind. Stretch your comfort zone following these principles.

◆ Every color is a good color, when used with harmonious companions.

◆ Each color around the color wheel actually represents a color family ranging from pale (light value) to very deep (dark value) and all the subtle variations in between.

◆ Contrast in value will give depth to your design and enrich whatever color harmony you choose.

Color Harmonies

Considering all the possible interpretations of each harmony in many color family combinations, you could make a lifetime of stunning quilts from following these five simple strategies. If you'd like to expand your color sense further, consult one of the excellent books listed in the resources, page 138.

Monochromatic

A monochromatic color scheme has only one color, usually in many shades or values, sometimes incorporating white or another neutral. Try any color around the wheel. ◆ To add liveliness to this soothing harmony, use equal amounts of light, medium, and dark values.

Analogous

Analogous means similar or related. Combine three colors that are side by side on the color wheel. Because the colors are close together, they will always blend in a pleasing way. Try yellow/yellow-green/green, blue-violet/violet/red-violet, or ANY adjacent colors. ◆ To spice up analogous color schemes, add an accent. Use one of the complements, across the color wheel from the analogous colors.

Complementary

Complementary colors are directly opposite each other on the color wheel. Every combination around the wheel will yield a rich, dynamic harmony in pastels or brights. Try yellow-orange/blue-violet or any other opposite pair. ◆ To add drama to this harmony, add a bit of an accent, two colors away from one of the complements.

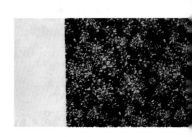

Split Complementary

A split complementary scheme features a color and the colors on either side of its complement. Think of a Y with its tail at the main color and its arms reaching to the split complementary colors. ◆ This combination is a bit more adventurous. Try red-violet/yellow/green or any other Y-combinations around the wheel.

Triadic

A triadic harmony incorporates three colors that are equally distant on the color wheel (three colors between). Try red-orange/yellow-green/blue-violet, or other triangles around the wheel. ◆ These vibrant and exciting harmonies may need some black or white for respite.

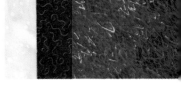

Complements

red	green
red-orange	blue-green
orange	blue
yellow-orange	blue-violet
yellow	violet
yellow-green	red-violet

Split Complements

red	yellow-green	blue-green
red-orange	green	blue
orange	blue-green	blue-violet
yellow-orange	blue	violet
yellow	blue-violet	red-violet
yellow-green	violet	red
green	red-violet	red-orange
blue-green	red	orange
blue	red-orange	yellow-orange
blue-violet	orange	yellow
violet	yellow-orange	yellow-green
red-violet	yellow	green

Triads

Primary colors:	red	yellow	blue
Secondary colors:	orange	green	violet
Tertiary colors:	red-orange	yellow-green	blue-violet
	yellow-orange	blue-green	red-violet

Cutting Piecing

Cutting Tips

◆ Always close the rotary cutter after EVERY stroke.

◆ Always cut AWAY from your body.

◆ Check your first cut strip to make sure the strip is straight.

◆ Check straight of grain every few strips as you continue to cut. Resquare the fabric as needed.

◆ If the strip of fabric to be cut is wider than your ruler, use two rulers to get the desired width.

◆ Do not cut through more than four layers of fabric. Cutting accuracy diminishes with each extra layer of fabric. Also, more stress is placed on the hands and wrists when cutting through increased layers of fabric.

◆ Many quilt blocks include triangles, which have extra large seam allowances at the tips. Unless otherwise directed, trim these "dog-ears" even with the 1/4" seam allowance of adjacent pieces after pressing and before stitching the next seam.

Rotary Cutting Basics

All the quilts in this book begin with cut strips of fabric. Cutting accurate and straight strips is the first secret to precision piecing in quiltmaking. See page 128 for essential tools.

Squaring Up the Fabric

Before cutting fabric, square up the uneven end so it is perpendicular to the fabric edge and all pieces will be cut on the straight grain.

1. Fold the fabric in half, selvage to selvage. Hold the fabric up to see if it hangs straight to the fold. If not, slide the layers a bit until the fabric hangs straight and selvages are together. It is important that the selvages are aligned and the folded edge is smooth.

2. Lay the fabric on the cutting mat with the folded edge closest to your body. Right-handed people should place the bulk of the fabric to their right. Left-handed people should place it to the left and reverse directions in the remaining instructions.

3. Fold the fabric in half again, bringing the fold up to meet the selvages. You will be cutting through four layers of fabric.

4. Line up your widest ruler precisely with the bottom fold, about 1/2" from the left edge of the fabric. Make sure all four layers of fabric extend beyond the left edge of the ruler.

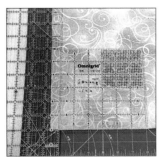

5. Line up a long ruler tight to the left edge of the wide ruler. Check that all four layers of fabric are under the long ruler.

6. Spread the fingertips of your left hand to apply even pressure on the long ruler. Remove the other ruler.

7. Using a rotary cutter, cut along the right edge of the long ruler, removing the uneven edge of all four layers of fabric with a single pass. Cut AWAY from your body.

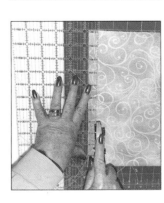

Cutting Strips and Shapes

To cut strips for strip-piecing or crosscutting into shapes, always make sure the fabric is square to begin. Check it every three or four cuts. If necessary, square the fabric again.

1. Line up the required measurement on the ruler with the cut straight edge of the fabric.
Measure carefully!
A Post-it note at the proper measurement on the ruler prevents errors.

2. Apply pressure with your fingertips on the ruler and make the cut with a single smooth pass of the rotary cutter. Cut AWAY from your body.

3. Crosscut the strips into squares or rectangles as called for in the pattern.

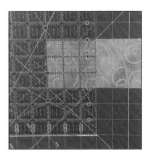

Make half-square triangles by cutting a square diagonally.

Make quarter-square triangles by cutting a square diagonally twice.

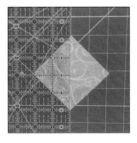

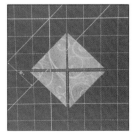

Stitching Basics

The quilts in this book use a scant 1/4" seam allowance. Sewing a scant 1/4" seam allowance is the second secret in precision piecing. Before you begin stitching your quilt top take a few minutes to check your scant 1/4" seam. See tips on page 129.

Set the stitch length to 12 stitches per inch. Use 100 percent cotton thread in a neutral color for light fabrics and a darker color for dark fabrics.

Pinning Pressing

Machine Piecing Techniques

Place two pieces of fabric with right sides together and raw edges aligned. Stitch the length of the raw edge in a scant 1/4" seam. Back-stitching is unnecessary because the seams will be crossed by other seams.

Begin and end each sewing sequence with a "starter." Stitch a small scrap of fabric under the presser foot, stopping at the front edge. This scrap is your starting point for the next seam. It saves time and thread while preventing small units from being drawn down into the throat plate.

Starter scrap saves time.

Strip-Piecing Techniques

Several quilts in this book call for piecing of fabric strips which are then crosscut into strips that become components of the final block.

1. Begin by arranging the pieces of fabric in the sequence stated in the pattern directions.

2. Line up the first two strips, matching the cut edges. Stitch.

3. Set the seam and press according to the directions.

4. If called for, add the next strip of fabric.

Chain-Piecing

Whenever possible, stitch all similar units in sequence, using the chain-piecing method:

1. Place fabric pieces to be joined under the presser foot and stitch the seam.

2. Take a few stitches with no fabric, then slide the next fabric pair under the toe of the presser foot. Do not lift the presser foot or clip the thread.

3. Take another few stitches with no fabric, then repeat with the next unit.

4. When all units have been sewn, end with your starter scrap.

5. Cut the stitched units from the starter and move to the ironing board for pressing.

6. Set and press the seams following the pressing arrows in the pattern.

7. Clip the units apart.

Slow down when stitching over intersecting seams

To make perfect points

When assembling units where one piece has intersecting seams, always pin before stitching.

Put the piece with the intersection on top so you can see clearly to sew exactly through the X intersection, even if the seam allowance will not be exactly 1/4".

To repair stitching errors

Use your seam ripper to "unsew" a seam when you've made a mistake.

◆ "Rip" every third stitch on one side of the fabric. Then gently lift the thread off the other side of the fabric.

◆ Remove ALL thread snippets before restitching the seam. If snippets do not come off easily, try masking tape.

Pinning

It is not necessary to pin long straight seams. However, it is advisable to pin when encountering seams and intersections that need to be lined up precisely.

To match intersecting seams

◆ Make sure seams are pressed in opposite directions.

◆ Wriggle the pieces together until the opposing seams nestle or "butt" together snugly. Peek to make sure the pieces are lined up.

◆ Place a pin in both sides of the intersecting seams.

◆ Stitch the seam slowly, removing the pins just before they come under the needle. Do not stitch over pins; doing so can bend or break the pin, cause broken needles, or throw off the timing of the sewing machine.

To match diagonal or multiple seams exactly

◆ Stab a pin vertically through the exact match point. Keep this pin standing upright to hold pieces in place. Do not pin it down.

◆ Pin the pieces together with a pin on both sides of the center pin. Remove the center pin.

SEAM
SEAMS MEET →
SEAM

Pressing

Pressing is the third secret to precision piecing. Press every fabric before cutting. Press each seam as you go. Look for the pressing arrows in the pattern diagrams and follow them for every step so that seam allowances at intersections are pressed in opposite directions to lie flat.

To press sewn units

◆ Start by "setting" the sewn seam. Place the sewn units or blocks on the ironing board with the seam facing away from your body. The fabric being "pressed toward" should be on top.

◆ Gently press the sewn seam, using a zigzag motion.

◆ Separate the two fabrics and fold the top fabric back over the seam allowances. Press gently.

For complicated designs, make a pressing plan so all seams butt—if possible—and you know which way to press them before you start. Within and between complex blocks, several seams may come together and prevent butting. If necessary, press these seams open.

133

Settings

Choosing a Setting

Making quilt blocks is only one-third of the quiltmaking process. The second phase is to decide on an attractive arrangement for the blocks and then assemble them into a quilt top. Blocks can be arranged into many settings:

◆ Straight (horizontal) set: blocks side by side in horizontal rows.

◆ Straight set with sashing: blocks side by side in horizontal rows with sashing (lattice) strips between the blocks.

◆ Diagonal (on-point) set: blocks turned 45° on their points and arranged in diagonal rows.

◆ Diagonal set with sashing: diagonal rows of blocks set on point with sashing (lattice strips) between the blocks.

◆ Alternate block setting: a plain block or a simple pieced block is substituted, checkerboard fashion, for half the blocks in a straight or diagonal setting.

◆ Strip setting: horizontal or vertical side-by-side placement of blocks in strips with plain fabric or strips of different blocks set between.

◆ Overall setting: single blocks placed in an arrangement so the pattern covers the entire quilt top.

◆ Medallion setting: large single block or group of blocks in the center of quilt.

Most of the quilts in this book use a straight-set pattern, but even within this simple setting there are unlimited possibilities for arranging blocks. Diagonally divided

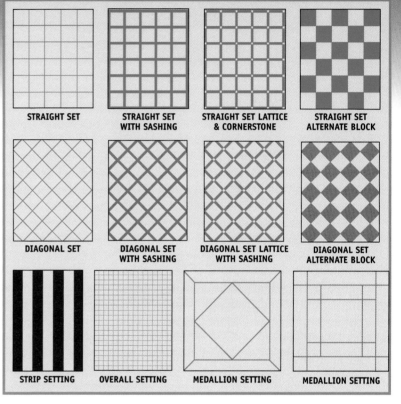

Read all instructions completely before beginning.

STRAIGHT SET	STRAIGHT SET WITH SASHING
STRAIGHT SET LATTICE & CORNERSTONE	STRAIGHT SET ALTERNATE BLOCK
DIAGONAL SET	DIAGONAL SET WITH SASHING
DIAGONAL SET LATTICE WITH SASHING	DIAGONAL SET ALTERNATE BLOCK
STRIP SETTING	OVERALL SETTING
MEDALLION SETTING	MEDALLION SETTING

light/dark blocks are especially versatile in creating intriguing designs across the quilt top.

For design inspiration, study examples of other settings scattered throughout this book. Pay attention to the settings in quilts you see and like. Then try them out with your latest project.

Experiment before Deciding

Use a design wall to play around with different block orientations and arrangements until you find one that fits your fabrics and artistic sensibilities. The results can be amazing.

Try turning your blocks diagonally for a lively design. King's Crown on point looks like a totally different block. Experiment with sashings between your blocks. Consider alternate block settings to show off very complex blocks, to make a larger quilt from a small number of blocks, or when you want to feature intricate machine or hand quilting in the plain blocks.

Don't be surprised if a different setting begs for a sashing fabric or border you didn't imagine beforehand. Stay open to the creative inspirations that emerge in this important second design phase of quiltmaking.

Sashings

Settings with sashing (lattice) strips were rare before the advent of the sewing machine which could stitch the long straight seams with ease. Today, quilters typically consider sashings as a design element in four situations:

◆ To provide unity in a quilt whose blocks are of varying sizes or disparate fabrics, especially in sampler quilts or when setting antique, appliquéd, or embroidered quilt blocks.

◆ To "stretch" a quilt to a larger size.

◆ To frame larger blocks for a "country" feel.

◆ To echo design elements in the quilt block.

Sashing strips can be set with squares at block intersections, or treated as quilt-wide

strips. Sashing strip width should be proportional to the elements in the blocks and replicate some feature in the block, if possible. See Crazy Quilt (pages 68–73) for step-by-step instructions to make sashings with setting squares. For a smooth, flat quilt top, press seams of setting squares toward the sashing.

Plan Ahead

Quilts that are set diagonally or with lattice strips take some extra planning before purchasing and cutting fabric. See instructions opposite for determining fabric requirements and cutting the essential corner and side setting triangles for on-point quilts.

Quilt Assembly

Once you have decided on a setting arrangement, it is time to assemble the quilt top. A design wall is helpful to keep blocks in order.

Straight (Horizontal) Set Quilt Assembly

◆ Lay out the blocks side by side in rows.

◆ Sew the blocks together in horizontal rows. Butt and pin all intersecting seams before sewing.

◆ Press as you go. Press all seams between blocks in the even rows to the right and all seams between blocks in the odd rows to the left.

◆ Lay out the completed rows.

◆ Sew the rows together from top to bottom. Butt and pin all seams before sewing.

◆ To prevent distortion when sewing the rows together, reverse sewing direction row by row. Sew Row 1 and Row 2 together stitching from left to right. Sew Row 3 to Row 2, stitching from right to left. Continue in this manner, alternating stitching direction until all the rows are sewn together.

◆ Press as you add each row. Press all seams in the same direction.

Diagonal (On-Point) Set Quilt Assembly

To finish the edges of quilts set on point (diagonally), side setting triangles and corner triangles are needed. These triangles can be half blocks from the pattern or cut from squares of the background fabric (see below).

◆ Lay out the blocks diagonally (on point) using the setting triangles to fill in the spaces around the edges of the quilt.

◆ Pin and sew the blocks and setting triangles together, one diagonal row at a time, pressing as you go. Press all seams between blocks in the even rows to the right and all seams between blocks in the odd rows to the left.

◆ Once the rows are assembled, sew the rows together from one corner to the opposite corner. Leave the corner triangles for last. Butt and pin all seams before sewing. Side setting triangles may be a bit larger than needed, but do not trim them until the whole quilt is assembled.

◆ To prevent distortion when sewing the rows together, reverse sewing direction row by row. Sew Row 1 and Row 2 together stitching from left to right. Sew Row 3 to Row 2, stitching from right to left. Continue in this manner, alternating stitching direction until all the rows are sewn together.

◆ Press seams between rows as you go. Press toward shorter row.

◆ Add the corner triangles last.

◆ Trim edges of the quilt evenly, maintaining a 1/4" seam allowance at the corners of blocks for adding the border.

Setting Triangles for Diagonal Settings

To stabilize the edge of the quilt, CORNER setting triangles are cut as half-square triangles, straight grain of the fabric on the short, outer legs of the triangle.

SIDE setting triangles are cut as quarter-square triangles, straight grain of the fabric on the long edge of the triangle, which becomes the edge of the quilt. The number of side setting triangles needed is determined by the number of blocks in the quilt.

Calculating corner and side setting triangle sizes

The size of the corner and side setting triangles is determined by the block size, using the magic geometric formulas to the right.

CORNER Setting Triangles

◆ DIVIDE the FINISHED size of the block by 1.4142. Round up to the nearest 1/8".

◆ Add 7/8" for seam allowances.

◆ Cut a square of your chosen fabric to that size. Cut the square in half diagonally once to make half-square triangles.

◆ The straight of the grain will be on the short sides of the triangles, the outside of the quilt.

SIDE Setting Triangles

◆ Determine the number of side setting triangles needed. Divide this number by four and round up to calculate the number of squares required.

◆ MULTIPLY the FINISHED size of the block by 1.4142. Round up to the nearest 1/8".

◆ Add 1 1/4" for seam allowances. This is the size square you will need for setting triangles. Calculate how much of your chosen fabric you will need to cut the number of squares required for your quilt size.

◆ Cut the required number of squares of your chosen fabric to that size. You may need two rulers side by side to cut these large squares. Cut the squares in half diagonally TWICE to make quarter-square triangles.

◆ The straight of the grain will be on the long side of the triangles, the outside of the quilt.

◆ Depending on the number of blocks in the quilt, there may be side setting triangles left over.

Finishing

Borders

The last step in making the quilt top is adding one or more borders to frame your creation. Many quilters do not decide on border treatment until the top is finished and they can see the total effect of the overall design.

Consider what type of borders might enhance your quilt. Choose one or more border types.

Inner borders are usually narrow (1/2"–2" finished). The first inner border frames the quilt and gives it definition. Consider a dark color or bold accent.

The **outer** border has nearly as much visual impact as the entire quilt top, so choose carefully. If you use the focus fabric from your blocks as a border, keep the border narrow (3"–5") so it doesn't overwhelm the top.

Plain, straight-set borders (the easiest for beginners) are attached to the sides first and then top and bottom. They are the most economical, especially when they are set with contrasting cornerstones.

Mitered borders take a bit more fabric and sewing expertise to make the Y-corners.

Pieced borders incorporate patchwork elements that coordinate with pieced blocks in the top. Pieced borders require considerable advance planning and may take as much time to assemble as the entire top.

For simplicity of presentation, instructions for all of the quilts in this book call for plain, straight-set borders, cut on the crosswise grain for economy. The inner border is usually 1"–2" finished. The outer border is usually 4" finished.

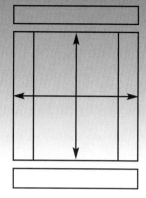

Making Plain (Straight-Set) Borders

Add side borders first

◆ Measure the quilt from top to bottom at the midpoint. Spread it out on the floor or a large table. Pull taut, but do not stretch.

◆ Cut two borders to this measurement.

For borders longer than 42", join two or more border strips together with diagonal seams.

◆ Pin the side borders. Divide the quilt side edge and the border strip into four equal sections, placing pins to mark the measurements: one in the midpoint, and one each, halfway between the midpoint and the ends of the border. Match the center pin of the quilt top to the center pin of the border strip and match the other two pins in a similar manner.

Use as many other pins as necessary.

◆ Stitch the side borders to the quilt.

For the innermost border, sew with the quilt on top so you can see to stitch through intersecting seams in the blocks. For subsequent borders, stitch with the border piece on top.

◆ Press the seams toward the border strips.

Add top and bottom borders

◆ Measure the width of the quilt at its center, including the side borders.

◆ Cut two borders to this measurement.

If necessary, piece long strips with diagonal seams.

◆ Pin and sew borders to top and bottom, following the process outlined for side borders.

Any additional borders are added in this same manner.

Finishing the Quilt

Once the borders are attached, the quilt top is finished and the final phase begins: making a quilt sandwich of top, batting, and backing, attaching the layers together with decorative hand or machine stitching, and finishing the quilt with binding and label.

Backing

For the backing layer, use all-cotton fabric, cut according to the backing layouts included with each pattern. Preshrink the backing fabric and cut off the selvage edges before cutting the backing. Use a 5/8" seam allowance when combining pieces for the backing and press the seam open.

Batting

Batting provides stability, depth, warmth, and dimension to a quilt. There are many different materials and brands of batting available. Ask for advice from experienced quilters. Open batting and allow it to relax overnight before sandwiching it in the quilt.

Professional Quilters

Many quilters enjoy designing and piecing tops more than quilting the layers together. In most areas of the country, professional machine quilters with special equipment offer their services to busy quilters. Check your local quilt shop for people in your region who will be happy to finish your quilt for you. Expect a six-month or more wait to get on the schedule. There are also many mail-order machine quilting services.

When you send a quilt out for machine quilting, be sure to cut the backing at least 4" larger than the top on ALL sides. Industrial machines need the extra inches to secure the quilt.

Cindy Provencher hand guides her Millennium quilting machine.

Making the Quilt Sandwich

If you decide to do your own quilting, begin by assembling the three quilt layers. If you have access to a quilt frame and experienced helpers, layer and baste your quilt that way. If not, try this home-style method.

◆ Cut batting and backing at least 3" larger than the quilt top on ALL sides.

◆ Lay the backing fabric, right side down, on a large, clean flat surface. Use masking tape to hold the backing tautly to the work surface.

◆ Spread the batting on top of the backing, smoothing it to make sure all the wrinkles are out.

◆ Lay the quilt top, right side up, on top of the batting. Smooth out any wrinkles and remove any stray threads.

The quilt sandwich is ready to baste.

Basting

Basting holds the three layers of the quilt together to prevent shifting during the quilting process.

For hand quilting, baste using a light colored thread, a long needle and a long running stitch. Start at the center of the quilt and baste in a grid horizontally and then vertically. The basting rows should be evenly spaced and about 4" apart.

For machine quilting, pin baste using #2 size safety pins. Start at the center of the quilt and work out, placing the pins approximately every 4".

Shelly and Barb pin baste their spool quilt.

Quilting

Quilting is the process used to hold the three layers of the quilt together without slipping. The simplest form of quilting is to **tie the layers together** with decorative thread, spacing the double square knots six inches apart or less. This process is much easier with a quilt frame, but quilters over the years have used the backs of chairs as supports.

Soup Group members tying a quilt.

Hand and machine quilting enhance the beauty of a quilt by adding texture and design. If you have never tried quilting, here are a few guidelines to get started.

Hand quilting features evenly spaced stitches in a predetermined pattern or design across the quilt top and/or within blocks. Use 18" lengths of 100 percent waxed cotton thread made especially for hand quilting in a color that matches or compliments your quilt design.

Always work from the center of the quilt to an outside edge. Try to make even stitches rather than small ones. See page 138 for excellent books on hand quilting methods.

Shirley and Carol Jean hand quilt a raffle quilt.

Machine quilting requires the use of an even-feed or walking foot for straight line quilting. A darning foot is used for free-motion quilting. Consult your machine instruction manual for information on tension settings. Use 100 percent cotton or one of the myriad of specialty threads on the market today.

Start in the center of the quilt and work toward the edges, rolling and unrolling the quilt as needed. For beginners, try straight lines 3" or less apart in a horizontal/vertical or diagonal grid. Or stitch in the ditch following seam lines between or within blocks. For more sophisticated machine quilting ideas, read one of the outstanding books on quilting recommended in the resources section, page 139.

Machine quilting tools and techniques.

Adding a Sleeve

If your quilt will be displayed on a wall or in a show, it needs a hanging sleeve made of muslin or leftover backing fabric

◆ Cut fabric 9" wide and 1" shorter than the width of the top edge of the quilt.

◆ Hem the short ends by turning under 1/2", than 1/2" again. Stitch.

◆ With WRONG sides together, fold the fabric in half lengthwise. Stitch with a 1/4" seam allowance.

◆ Baste the raw edge of the sleeve to the top edge of the quilt back BEFORE the binding is added. The sleeve will be secured when the binding is sewn onto the quilt.

◆ To finish the sleeve, push the bottom edge of the sleeve up about an inch and blind stitch the bottom of the sleeve to the quilt back.

more ➔

Finishing

Binding

Binding finishes the edge of the quilt after it has been quilted. Trim the excess batting and backing from the quilt sandwich first. The quilts in this book all used straight grain strips cut 2 1/4" wide. If available, use your machine's walking foot to sew on binding.

1. Measure the perimeter of your quilt to determine the needed length of binding. Add 12" for a safety margin.
2. To get the desired length of binding piece several 2 1/4" strips together using diagonal seams. Press the seams open and trim.
3. Fold the strips lengthwise with wrong sides together. Press.
4. At one end, unfold the binding and turn under 1/4" at a 45° angle. Pin to secure temporarily.

5. Beginning 2" from the pinned starting point, stitch the binding to the quilt with a 1/4" seam allowance.

6. Stitch to within 1/4" of the first corner. Stop and backstitch.

7. To miter the corner, fold the binding up and away from the quilt, forming a 45° angle.

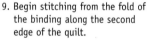

10. Repeat this process at each corner.
11. When you reach the beginning of the binding, cut the end you are sewing about 1" longer than needed and tuck the end inside the beginning. Complete the final stitching.

8. Fold the binding down.

9. Begin stitching from the fold of the binding along the second edge of the quilt.

12. Turn the binding to the back, folding it over the raw edges of the quilt. Blind stitch in place on the quilt back.

13. At each corner, fold the binding to form miters and blind stitch to secure.

Preserving Your Quilt

To preserve and prolong the life of your quilts, treat them with TLC.

◆ Keep them out of direct sunlight.

◆ Refold quilts often to prevent creases and fabric strain.

◆ Beware of changes in temperature and humidity.

◆ Never store quilts in plastic bags.

Quilt Label

When the quilt is finished, sign and date it on the back, lower right-hand corner, using a permanent pen. Or make a label that can be hand stitched to the back.

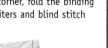

138

Suggested Reading

Basic Quilting

Anderson, Alex. *Start Quilting with Alex Anderson.* Lafayette, CA: C&T Publishing, 1997.

Doak, Carol. *Your First Quilt Book (Or It Should Be!).* Bothell, WA: That Patchwork Place, 1997.

Hargrave, Harriet and Sharyn Craig. *The Art of Classic Quiltmaking.* Lafayette, CA: C&T Publishing, 2000.

Kough, Lynn G. *Quiltmaking for Beginners: A Stitch-by-Stitch Guide to Hand and Machine Techniques.* Lincolnwood, IL: The Quilt Digest, 2000.

Pahl, Ellen, ed. *The Quilters Ultimate Visual Guide: From A to Z — Hundreds of Tips and Techniques for Successful Quiltmaking.* Emmaus, PA: Rodale Press, 1997.

Borders and Settings

Craig, Sharyn. *Setting Solutions.* Lafayette, CA: C&T Publishing, 2001.

Martin, Judy and Marsha McClosky. *Pieced Borders: The Complete Resource.* Grinnell, IA: Crosley-Griffith Publishing Company Inc, 1994.

Miller, Phyllis D. *Sets & Sashings for Quilts.* Paducah, KY: American Quilter's Society, 2000.

Schneider, Sally, ed. *Sensational Sets & Borders.* Emmaus, PA: Rodale Press, 1998.

Color and Fabric Selection

Anderson, Alex. *Fabric Shopping with Alex Anderson.* Lafayette, CA: C&T Publishing, 2000.

Barnes, Christine. Color: *The Quilter's Guide.* Bothell, WA: That Patchwork Place, 1997.

Beyer, Jinny. *Color Confidence for Quilters.* Lincolnwood, IL: The Quilt Digest Press, 1992.

Penders, Mary Coyne. *Color and Cloth.* Lincolnwood, IL: The Quilt Digest Press, 1995.

Wolfrom, Joen. *Color Play.* Lafayette, CA: C&T Publishing, 2000.

Crazy Quilts

Causee, Linda. *Learn to Make a Crazy Quilt*. San Marcos, CA: American School of Needlework, 1998.

Causee, Linda. *101 Crazy Quilt Blocks*. San Marcos, CA: American School of Needlework, 2001.

Michler, J. Marsha. *Crazy Quilts by Machine*. Iola, WI: Krause Publications, 2000.

Michler, J. Marsha. *The Magic of Crazy Quilting*. Iola, WI: Krause Publications, 1998.

Montano, Judith Baker. *Elegant Stitches: An Illustrated Stitch Guide & Source Book of Inspiration*. Lafayette, CA: C&T Publishing, 1995.

Finishing

Dunn, Sarah Sachs, ed. *Fantastic Finishes*. Emmaus, PA: Rodale Press, 1999.

Dietrich, Mimi. *Happy Endings: Finishing the Edges of Your Quilt*. Bothell, WA: That Patchwork Place, 1987.

Mazuran, Cody. *A Fine Finish*. Bothell, WA: That Patchwork Place, 1997.

Hand and Machine Quilting

Anderson, Alex. *Hand Quilting with Alex Anderson*. Lafayette, CA: C&T Publishing, 1998.

Hargrave, Harriet. *Heirloom Machine Quilting*. Lafayette, CA: C&T Publishing, 1990.

Kimball, Jeana. *Loving Stitches*. Bothell, WA: That Patchwork Place, 1992.

Nelson, Suzanne, et al. *Flawless Hand Quilting*. Emmaus, PA: Rodale Press, 1999.

Noble, Maurine. *Machine Quilting Made Easy*. Bothell, WA: That Patchwork Place, 1994.

Simms, Ami. *How to Improve Your Quilting Stitch*. Flint, MI: Mallery Press, 1996.

Squire, Helen. *Helen's Copy & Use*. Paducah, KY: American Quilter's Society, 2002.

Townswick, Jane, ed. *Easy Machine Quilting*. Emmaus, PA: Rodale Press, 1996.

Leone, Diana and Cindy Walter. *Fine Hand Quilting*, 2nd edition. Iola, WI: Krause Publications, 2000.

Wallner, Hari. *Trapunto by Machine*. Lafayette, CA: C&T Publishing, 1996.

Machine Appliqué

Hargrave, Harriet. *Mastering Machine Appliqué*, 2nd edition. Lafayette, CA: C&T Publishing, 2001.

Nickels, Sue. *Machine Appliqué: A Sampler of Techniques*. Paducah, KY: American Quilter's Society, 2001.

Noble, Maurine. *Basic Quiltmaking Techniques for Machine Appliqué*. Bothell, WA: That Patchwork Place, 1998.

Soltys, Karen Costello, ed. *Appliqué Made Easy*. Emmaus, PA: Rodale Press, 1998.

Machine and Hand Piecing

Collins, Sally. *The Art of Machine Piecing*. Lafayette, CA: C&T Publishing, 2001.

Soltys, Karen Costello, ed. *Perfect Piecing*. Emmaus, PA: Rodale Press, 1997.

Thomas, Donna Lynn. *A Perfect Match: A Guide to Precise Machine Piecing*. Bothell, WA: That Patchwork Place, 1998.

Foundation and Paper Piecing

Anderson, Alex. *Paper Piecing with Alex Anderson*. Lafayette, CA: C&T Publishing, 2002.

Causee, Linda. *Learn to Make a Foundation-Pieced Quilt*. San Marcos, CA: American School of Needlework, 1998.

Doak, Carol. *Easy Machine Paper Piecing*. Bothell, WA: That Patchwork Place, 1994.

Hall, Jane and Dixie Haywood. *Precision Pieced Quilts Using the Foundation Method*. Radnor, PA: Chilton Book Company, 1992.

Pressing

Giesbrecht, Myrna. *Press for Success: Secrets for Precise and Speedy Quiltmaking*. Bothell, WA: That Patchwork Place, 1999.

Quilt Block Construction and History

Beyer, Jinny. *The Quilter's Album of Blocks & Borders*. McLean, VA: EPM Publications, 1980, 1986.

Brackman, Barbara. *Encyclopedia of Pieced Quilt Patterns*. Paducah, KY: American Quilter's Society, 1993.

Finley, Ruth E. *Old Patchwork Quilts and the Women Who Made Them*. McLean, VA: EPM Publications, 1929, 1957.

Havig, Bettina. *Carrie Hall Blocks: over 800 historical patterns*. Paducah, KY: American Quilter's Society, 1999.

Kansas City Star. *One Piece at a Time: A Selection of the Legendary Kansas City Star Patterns*. Kansas City, MO: Kansas City Star Books, 1999.

Martin, Judy. *The Block Book*. Grinnell, IA: Crosley-Griffith Publishing Company Inc, 1998.

Rotary Cutting

Anderson, Alex. *Rotary Cutting*. Lafayette, CA: C&T Publishing, 1999.

Dunn, Sarah Sacks, ed. *Rotary Cutting & Speed Piecing*. Emmaus, PA: Rodale Press, 2000.

Johnson-Srebro, Nancy. *Rotary Magic*. Emmaus, PA: Rodale Press, 1997.

McClosky, Marsha. *Guide to Rotary Cutting*. Seattle, WA: Feathered Star Productions, 1990, 1993.

Poster, Donna. *The Quilter's Guide to Rotary Cutting*, 2nd ed. Iola, WI: Krause Publications, 1999.

Thomas, Donna Lynn. *Shortcuts: A Concise Guide to Rotary Cutting*. Bothell, WA: Martingale & Company, 1999.

Quilting Organizations

American Quilter's Society
P. O. Box 3290, Paducah, KY 42002
270-898-7903
aqsquilt@apex.net

National Quilting Association
P. O. Box 393,
Ellicott City, MD 21041
410-461-5733
www.his.com/queenb/nqa

International Quilting Association
7660 Woodway, Suite 550,
Houston, TX 77063
713-781-6864
iqa@quilts.com

Selected Publications

American Patchwork and Quilting (bimonthly)
800-677-4876
www.bhg.com/crafts

American Quilter (quarterly)
270-898-7903
www.aqsquilt.com

McCall's Quilting (bimonthly)
800-944-0736
www.mccallsquilting.com

The Quilter Magazine (7 times/year)
800-877-5527
www.thequiltermag.com

Quilter's Newsletter Magazine (monthly except Jan/Feb, Jul/Aug)
800-477-6089
www.quiltersnewsletter.com

Quilting Today (bimonthly)
570-278-1984
www.quilttownusa.com

Quiltmaker (bimonthly)
800-477-6089
www.quiltmaker.com

Traditional Quiltworks (bimonthly)
570-278-1984
www.quilttownusa.com

Professional Machine Quilters

Tami Bradley
Enchanted Desert Quilter
565 College Drive, Suite C130
Henderson, NV 89015
702-245-7464

Merry Ellestad & Rosemary Paur Walsberg
Quilting Up North
218 Third Avenue
Two Harbors, MN 55616
218-834-3268

Angela Haworth
Catalyst Threads
513-8th Avenue East
Superior, WI 54880
715-392-5133

Bonnie Jusczak
Pine Needle Quilting
3544 West Tischer Road
Duluth, MN 55803
218-728-6950

Sue Kahlberg
The Quilted Nook
10697 South Tracy Road
Solon Springs, WI 54873
715-378-2301

Cindy Larson
Country Roads Machine Quilting
32643 Camp Avenue
Vesta, MN 56292
507-762-3178

Karen McTavish
Superior Custom Machine Quilting
1748 Wildwood Road
Duluth, MN 55804
218-525-0103

Sue Munns
Sue's Quilt Studio
6632 Bergstrom Road
Duluth, MN 55803
218-722-3835

Carolyn Napper
Superior Stitches
10 Arthur Drive
Silver Bay, MN 55601
218-226-4441

Jan Peterson
Toni's Daughter
9226 East Cedar Avenue
Solon Springs, WI 54873
715-378-4399

Cindy Provencher
Cindy's Creative Quilting
319 North Central Avenue
Duluth, MN 55807
612-624-8337

Pam Schaefer
In Stitches
3572 County Road 8
P. O. Box 484
Moose Lake, MN 55767
218-389-6863

Jan Seidel
Quality Quilting by Jan
86255 Bark River Road
Herbster, WI 54844
715-774-3451

Pam Stolen
Mission Creek Quilting
13107 West Ninth Street
Duluth, MN 55808
218-626-3344

Helen Smith Stone
Skyline Quilting
415 East Skyline Parkway
Duluth, MN 55805
218-722-9880

Preparing for Mitering Corners

◆ Follow directions for measuring and making borders.

◆ Sew the three borders together.

◆ Press the side borders toward the outer border fabric.

◆ Press the top and bottom borders toward the inner border.

◆ Measure the border units and place a pin at the center and at exact edge as shown. (1)

◆ Place a pin at the exact center of the quilt.(1)

◆ Center and pin the top and bottom border sections to the quilt matching the center and the edge pins.(2)

◆ With the wrong side of the quilt up start and stop stitching within 1/4" of quilt edge.(2)

◆ Center and pin the side border sections to the quilt matching the center and the edge pins.

◆ With the wrong side of the quilt up start and stop stitching within 1/4" of quilt edge.

Mitering Corners

◆ Do not press the borders and the quilt yet.

◆ Fold the quilt diagonally as shown.(3)

◆ Butt the borders together. They should butt perfectly because they are pressed in different directions.

◆ Lay at least an 18–24" ruler along the diagonal fold. Place the 45° line on the ruler along the bottom edge of the borders as shown. Draw a line along the edge of the ruler.

◆ Pin the borders together and stitch on the drawn line. Always stitch from the outside edge and stop at the quilt edge.

◆ Trim seam allowance 1/4" from sewn line. Press seams open.

◆ Press the quilt and border junction in the direction of the borders.

You will be able to stitch directly through any point if the quilt portion is on the top.

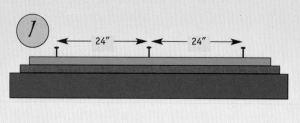

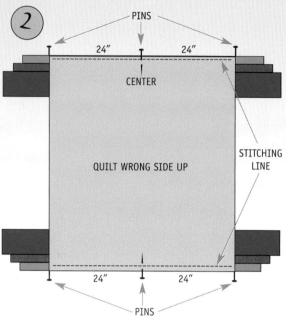

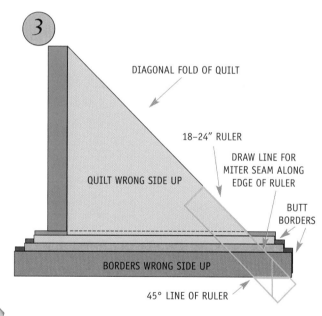

Always sew from outside edge toward the quilt. Stop stitching 1/4" from the quilt and take 2–3 backstitches.

Triangle Paper

Several quilts in this book, such as End of the Day and Next-Door Neighbor, lend themselves to the use of triangle paper. There are many different kinds of triangle paper on the market, but basically the directions are the same for all of them.

◆ Cut two pieces of fabric at least 1" larger than the grid.

◆ Place right sides of fabric together.

◆ Pin the grid paper to the wrong side of one of the fabrics.

◆ Reduce stitch length and stitch on the dashed lines.

◆ Cut on the solid lines.

◆ Remove paper and press triangle in accordance with pattern directions.

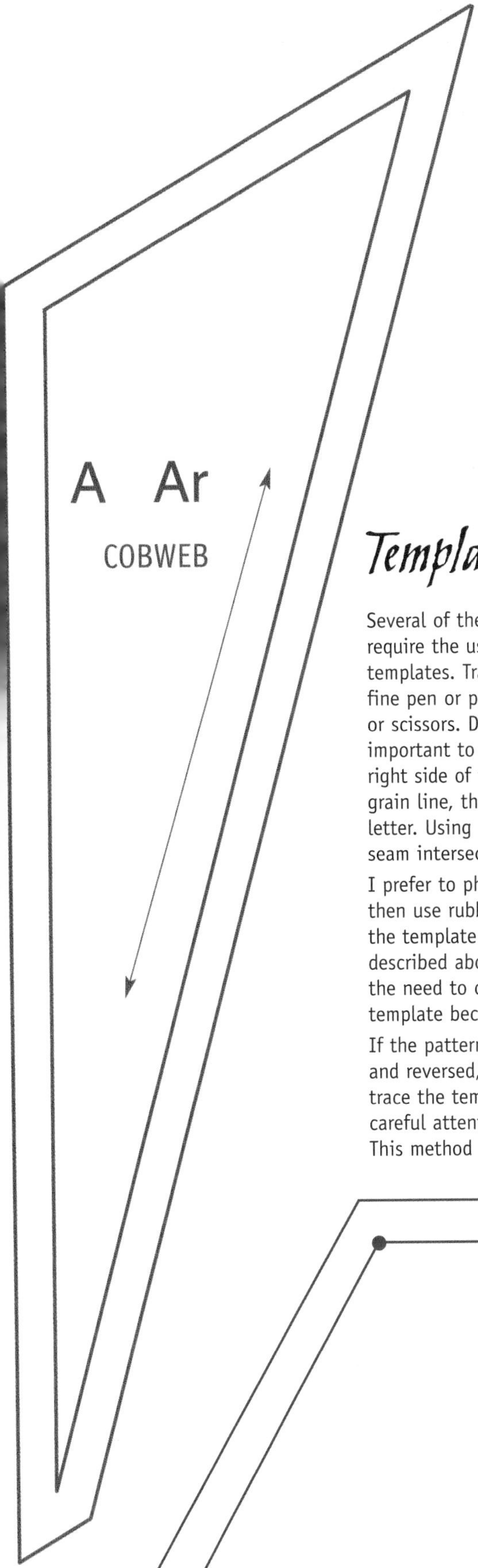

A Ar

COBWEB

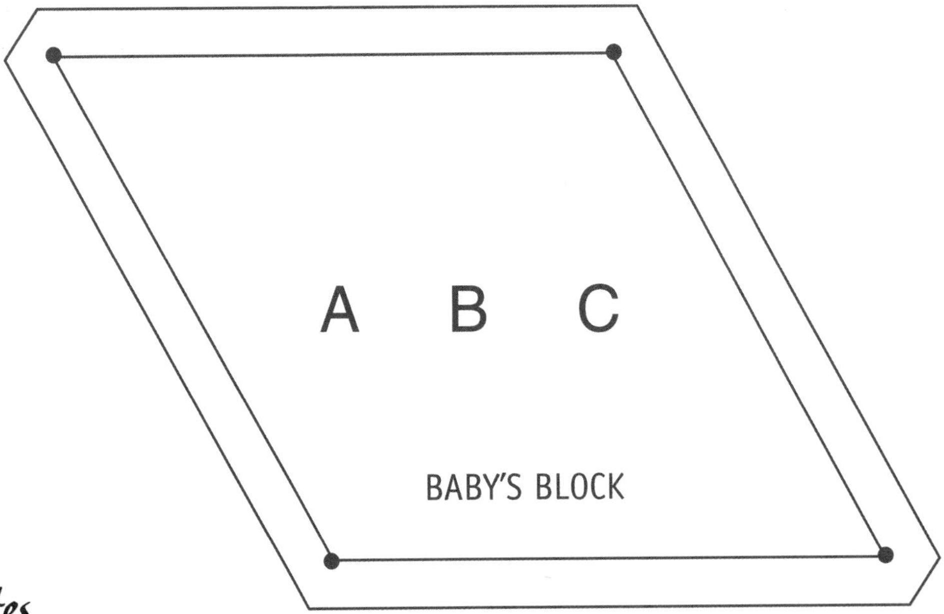

A B C

BABY'S BLOCK

E I

BABY'S
BLOCK

D F

BABY'S BLOCK

G H

BABY'S BLOCK

Templates

Several of the quilts in this book have odd-shaped pieces and require the use of templates. Patterns are provided for each of the templates. Trace each pattern piece onto template plastic using a fine pen or pencil. Cut the templates using either a rotary cutter or scissors. Do not use fabric scissors to cut plastic. It is important to trace and cut the template accurately. On the right side of the template mark the 1/4" seam lines, the grain line, the quilt name, and the pattern piece letter. Using a 1/16" hole punch, mark the seam intersections.

I prefer to photocopy the pattern piece and then use rubber cement to glue the pattern to the template plastic. I then cut the template as described above. This method is easy and eliminates the need to copy all the information onto the template because it is already there.

If the pattern calls for fabric pieces to be cut as shown and reversed, fold the fabric with right sides together and trace the template on the wrong side of the fabric. Pay careful attention to the grain line indicated on the template. This method gives you the template as pictured and reversed.

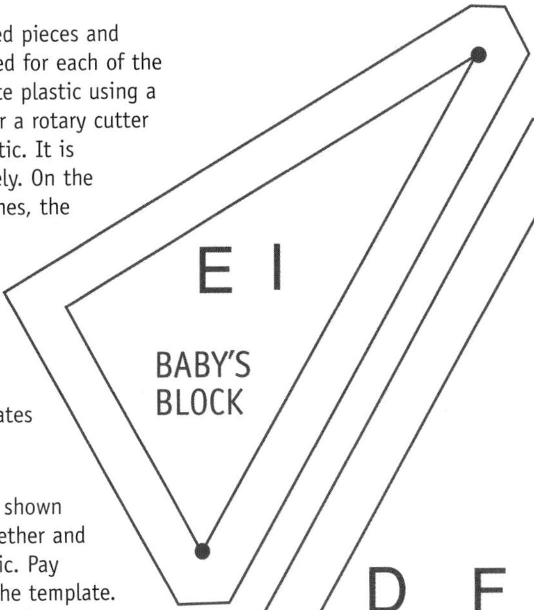

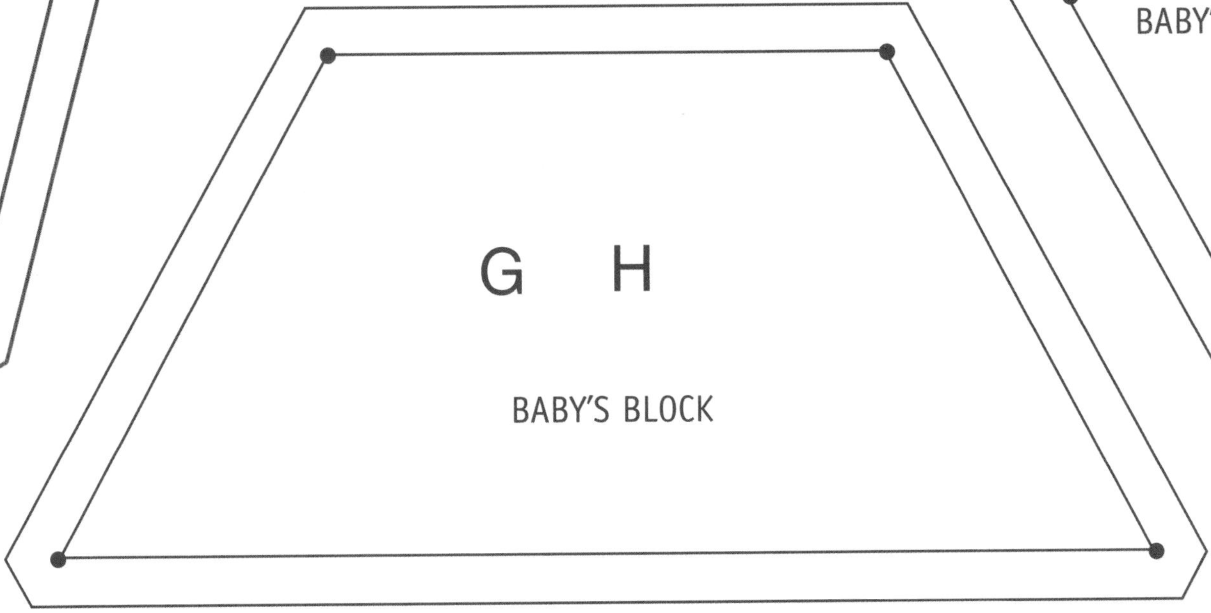

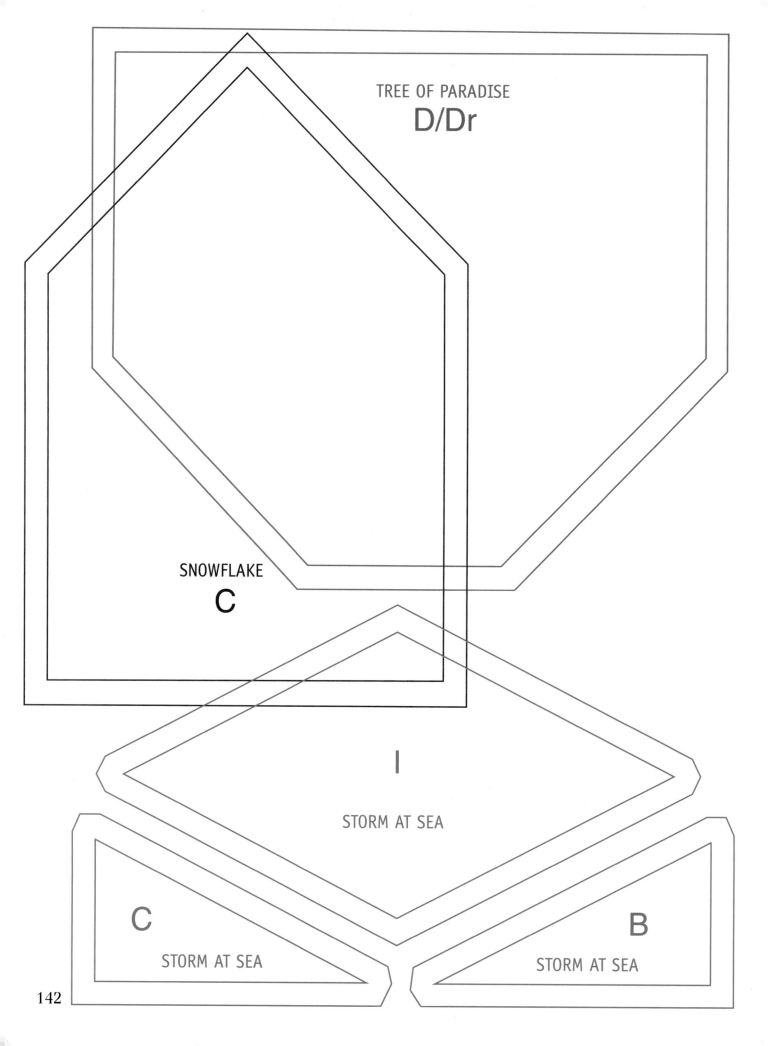

TREE OF PARADISE
D/Dr

SNOWFLAKE
C

I

STORM AT SEA

C

B

STORM AT SEA

STORM AT SEA

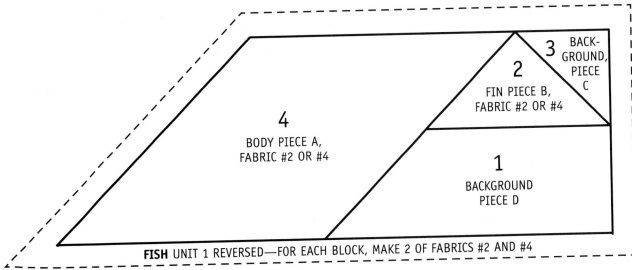

4
BODY PIECE A,
FABRIC #2 OR #4

2
FIN PIECE B,
FABRIC #2 OR #4

3
BACK-
GROUND,
PIECE
C

1
BACKGROUND
PIECE D

FISH UNIT 1 REVERSED—FOR EACH BLOCK, MAKE 2 OF FABRICS #2 AND #4

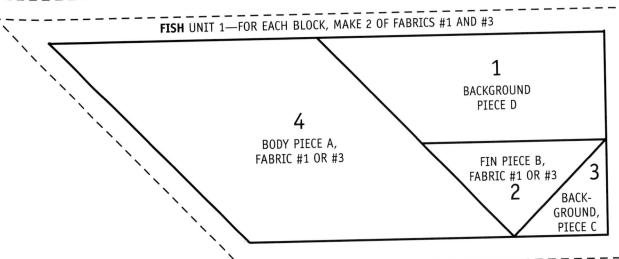

FISH UNIT 1—FOR EACH BLOCK, MAKE 2 OF FABRICS #1 AND #3

1
BACKGROUND
PIECE D

4
BODY PIECE A,
FABRIC #1 OR #3

2
FIN PIECE B,
FABRIC #1 OR #3

3
BACK-
GROUND,
PIECE C

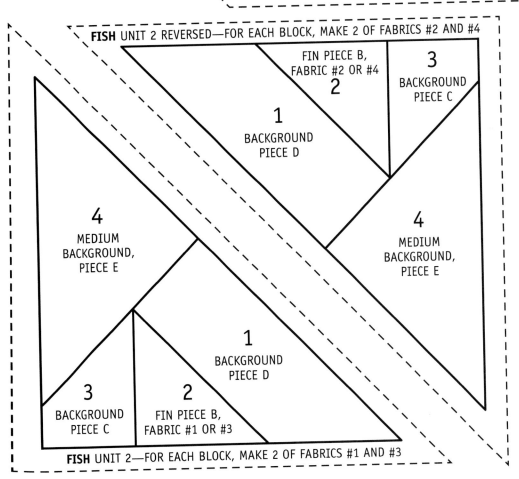

FISH UNIT 2 REVERSED—FOR EACH BLOCK, MAKE 2 OF FABRICS #2 AND #4

2
FIN PIECE B,
FABRIC #2 OR #4

3
BACKGROUND
PIECE C

1
BACKGROUND
PIECE D

4
MEDIUM
BACKGROUND,
PIECE E

4
MEDIUM
BACKGROUND,
PIECE E

1
BACKGROUND
PIECE D

3
BACKGROUND
PIECE C

2
FIN PIECE B,
FABRIC #1 OR #3

FISH UNIT 2—FOR EACH BLOCK, MAKE 2 OF FABRICS #1 AND #3

Acknowledgments

Our heartfelt thanks and gratitude to those who made this book possible:

Quiltmakers (page number of quilt)

Judy Beron(111), Marcia Bowker(37), Mary Bowker(37), Michelle Bowker(104), Maggie Brilla(55), Carol Jean Brooks(46), Lynne Chilberg(10), Carol Clark(49), Mary Eblom(113), Vicki Fosnacht(85), Toni Gotelaere(108), Lucy Hefti(49), Carol J. Hinz(49), LaVonne Horner(99), Joan Hunn(40), Diane Knudson(114), Ardis Leland(43), Andy Lien(31), Joanne Larsen Line(8,25,26,31,32,34,38,50, 64,70,73,81,82,92,126), Barbara McKeever(14,22,96), Shelly McKeever(14), Claudia Clark Myers(58), Rita Nau(63), Diane Nyman(90), Elaine Nyquist(49), Stephanie Orlowski(52), Kim Matteen Orlowski(89), Julie Owen(66,110), Ann Ketcham Palmer(93), Cindy Provencher(67), Joe Provencher(67), Lori Sandelin(9), Patricia Seeklander(49), Eileen Sugars(44), Danna Swenson(98), Sandy Thomson(107), Judy J. Timm(74,102), Jessica Torvinen(71), Austin Torvinen(71), Nancy Loving Tubesing(20,25,28), Kim Hoffmockel Wells(127), Marsha Wells(120), Brenda Willman(116), Dee Wojciehowski(53).

Machine quilters (page number of quilt)

Marcia Bowker(37,104), Tami Bradley(28), Merry Ellestad(16,22,85), Angela Haworth(55,64,66,81,92,96,110,113,126), Bonnie Jusczak(70), Sue Kallberg(98,102), Cindy Larson(49), Karen McTavish(32,38,50,74,82), Sue Munns(25,26,31,46), Claudia Clark Myers(71), Carolyn Napper(40,99), Rita Nau(63) Jan Peterson(13,34,44), Cindy Provencher(10,31,67,120,127), Pam Schaefer(8,20,93), Jan Seidel(25), Pam Stolan(52,89,90), Helen Smith Stone(56,73), Rosemary Paur Walsberg(16,22,85).

Mini-quilt makers

Nancy Andreae, Ruth Bartsch, Arlene Birchem, Kelly Bogrien, Mary Boman, Marcia Bowker, Michelle Bowker, Jean Brehmer, Carol Jean Brooks, Kristine Campbell, Jeanette Christensen, Patty Christensen, Mary Corbin, Mary Coy, Linda Dally, Marian Degnan, Claudia Dodge, Mary Eblom, Jill Ellsworth, Barb Engelking, Retta Fifo, Gail Fisher, Betty Firth, Donna Fleetwood, Toni Floyd, Linda Ford, Edna Georgious, Judy Gillen, Carol Goman, Joyce Gonzalez, Toni Gotelaere, Shari Guimont, Susan Gustafson, Cindy Hagen, Julie Hartmann, Peggy Hayes, Linda Johnson, Marlene Johnson, Rita Johnson, Rose Johnson, Shirley Kirsch, Joyce Knapp, Diane Knudson, Eileen Korpi, Cindy Koski, Ann Marden Krafthefer, Penny LaBerge, Agnes Lammi, Donna Lease, Ferne Liberty, Susan MacLennan, Bonnie Malterer, Susan Manning, Carol Maupins, Kim McFarlin, Barbara McKeever, Karen McTavish, Janet McTavish, Lisa Mesedahl, Jan Messner, Sue Munns, Claudia Clark Myers, Laura Nagel, Mona Nelson, Diane Nyman, Kim Matteen Orlowski, Ann Ketcham Palmer, Mary Ann Pelletier, Carolyn Peters, Clyda Prosen, Cindy Provencher, Mary Richard, Karren Robinson, Gail Ruuhela, Dorothy Schuknecht, Bev Solseng, Carol Soular, Eileen Sugars, Sandy Thomson, Judy J. Timm, Judy Trempe, Cheryl Wallace, Velda Weeks, Kim Hoffmockel Wells, Vonn Wien Wells, Sue Brooks Wiitanen, Elizabeth Wilhelmson, Vickie Youngquist-Smith.

Friendship Star quilt makers

Nancy Andreae, Ami Bieurance, Jean Bouen, Marcia Bowker, Jeanette Christensen, Mary Coy, Gail de Marcken, Marion Degnan, Pat Doran, Nancy Elmore, Jill Ellsworth, Donna Fleetwood, Toni Floyd, Linda Ford, Toni Gotelaere, Shari Guimont, Susan Gustafson, Cindy Hagen, Mavis Harmon, Julie Hartmann, Ann Higgins, Maxine Jacks, Liz Benson Johnson, Rose Johnson, Shirley Kirsch, Joyce Knapp, Cindy Koski, Karen Lamppa, Susan Manning, Kim McFarlin, Lisa Mesedahl, Mona Nelson, Sharon Nemec, Ann Ketcham Palmer, Clyda Prosen, Judy Rich, Pearl Riesgraf, Barb Rinne, Gail Ruuhela, Melodee Schreffler, Dorothy Schuknecht, Brenda Shock, Karen Skraba, Bev Solseng, Carol Soular, Vicki Strommen, Eileen Sugars, Judy Trempe, Velda Weeks, Vickie Youngquist-Smith.

Soup Group Quilters

Dottie Aitchison, Mary Boman, Carol Jean Brooks, Jane Carnes, Betty Firth, Vicki Fosnacht, Peggy Hayes, Pam Iverson, Shirley Kirsch, Ferne Liberty, Joanne Larsen Line, Barb McKeever, Sue Munns, Bev Semmelroth, Barb Skogg, Mae Wickland.

Graphic artist

Joy Morgan Dey for her book and cover design, diagram drafting, flexibility, creativity, and personal support throughout the process of creating *More Quilts from The Quiltmaker's Gift.*

Snapshot photographers

Joy Morgan Dey, Don McKeever, Tom Myers, Barbara Skogg.

Proofreaders

Lila Taylor Scott, Susan Gustafson.

Glossary & Index

(page references in parentheses)

Accent
Small amount of unexpected color in a block or quilt. Usually one of the colors nearly opposite the main color on the color wheel. (131)

Alternate Plain Block
Block made out of a whole piece of fabric that is placed between stitched blocks. (134–135)

Alternate Design Block
Pieced or appliquéd block that is placed between the main stitched blocks. (134–135)

Backing
Large piece of fabric that covers the back of a quilt. Bottom layer of the quilt sandwich. Backing may be seamed together from more than one piece of fabric. (136)

Background Fabric
Fabric of contrasting value to fabric of main design elements in quilt block. Usually a neutral or light color, occasionally dark.

Batting
A layer sandwiched inside the quilt, between the top and the backing. Usually made of a fluffy polyester, cotton, or wool which adds warmth and texture to the quilt. (136)

Bias
The diagonal of a woven fabric, which runs at a 45° angle to the selvage. Bias is very stretchy. Pieces cut on the bias need to be handled and pressed carefully to prevent stretching. (130)

Binding
A doubled strip of fabric, cut on either the straight of grain or the bias. Stitched to the edge of a quilt to cover the raw edges of the three layers. (138)

Block
Usually a square or rectangle design unit that is pieced or appliquéd. Typically, quilt tops are made by repeating one or more quilt block designs in a pleasing arrangement.

Border
One or more strips of fabric or patchwork surrounding the main body of the quilt top like the frame on a picture. May be pieced or appliquéd. Many quilts have borders of varying widths. (136)

Botanicals
Fabrics featuring actual or abstract images of nature: leaves, grass, trees, wood grain, etc.

Butting
When seam allowances of intersecting seams fall in opposite directions so they nestle closely together and seams line up on the right side. Sometimes referred to as nesting. (133)

Chain Piecing
Technique used to sew units together, one after another, without lifting the presser foot or cutting the thread between them. (133)

Complement
Color directly opposite on the color wheel. (131)

Corner Square
A square of fabric sometimes used to join adjacent border strips.

Corner Triangle
A half-square triangle used to fill in the four corners of a diagonally set quilt before borders are added. (135)

Cornerstone
See Setting Square.

Crosscut
In rotary cutting, the second cut, dividing a fabric strip or strip set into squares, rectangles, or strips of precise measurement. (132)

Crosswise grain
Threads of a fabric that are woven from selvage to selvage. Crosswise grain has some stretch. (130)